Remembering Judith

BY RUTH JOSEPH

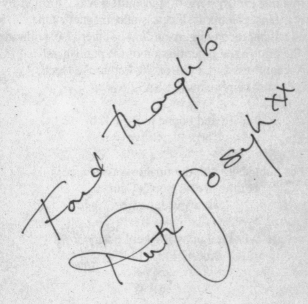

Fond Thoughts

Ruth Joseph xx

Published by Accent Press Ltd - 2005
ISBN 1905170017
Copyright © Ruth Joseph 2005

Printed and bound in the UK by
Clays Plc, St Ives

Published with the financial assistance
of the Welsh Books Council
www.gwales.com

Cover Design by Rachel Loosmore
Accent Press Ltd

To Judith

Acknowledgements

A sincere thank you to Hazel Cushion and Rachel Loosmore of Accent Press, who took me under their wing and are always friendly, positive and encouraging, Catherine Merriman my editor and friend for doing such a superb job on this book, Tony Burke from the Welsh National Opera library and my special husband and family.

Ah think then, sweet people, when you look on us, clad in our motley and tinsel, ours are human hearts, beating with passion, we are but men like you. For gladness or sorrow, 'tis the same broad Heaven above us, the same wide lonely world before us! Will ye hear, then, the story? How it unfolds...

From the Prologue of Pagliacci

Foreword

Your bloody memory taps you on the shoulder when your back is turned. Smell that perfume. Remember when your mother used to wear it?

I am small. About four years old. A scene many of you who were children in the 50's will remember. She's off to a party. She's promised she'll show me her dress. I lie in my bed waiting, it seems, for hours. Then she pushes open my door and wakes up the dark with a rustle of taffeta, a swish of silk and a mist of perfume.

'Let's see, Mummy – let's see! Please, put the light on.'

She laughs a tinkling sound, not her usual laugh, but in her special other-people voice. She moves to the switch and, suddenly, the room is neon-bright. I blink, rub my eyes, unaccustomed to its dazzle, and she is standing there like a film star, blond hair set in rigid Marcel waves curling into her slim face, her narrow pale shoulders exposed above folds of shot fabric. Her skirt is decorated with appliqué leaves and flowers, and she twirls on six-inch crocodile platform shoes. She is beautiful. But the vision lasts only seconds. The warmth, the laughter, is gone with a 'Sweetheart, you must go to sleep now'. She leans over the bed planting a dark-red kiss and laughs when it marks my cheek, rubbing the smear with a red-nailed finger. Then she is gone and I am back in the black, and the dressing gown returns to the face of a witch, the man in the moon laughs through the curtained window, and the monsters under the bed sharpen their claws to catch me if I dare dangle a foot.

But later, much later, I hear shouts from their bedroom. They are arguing and I can hear her sobbing – it begins as muffled whimpers and intermittent cries like the yelping of a lost puppy. But she often cried – that's what girls do, isn't it? The sound becomes louder, and now he is screaming indistinguishable words at her. I call and call. Nobody comes. The monsters are flexing their talons and won't let me get out of bed. So I sing to try to drown their scratching and the bad from that room, with a high-pitched lisping of a repertoire repeated from *Music While You Work*. Then I'm Wilfred Pickles, muttering in a broad north-country accent to 'Give 'em the money Mabel'. Eventually, I fall asleep.

In the morning, I sit with our mother's help in the breakfast room. She's made me some porridge. I never like it when she makes it. It is decorated with black bitter flecks. It lies crouching in a blue and white striped dish like a grey solid mound surrounded by a moat of luke-warm milk and topped with a scab of brown sugar crust. I'm excavating broken lumps swimming round the bowl, trying to force the stuff down, concentrating on *Housewives Choice*, which is playing 'Spanish Eyes' and selections from the 'Desert Song' to busy ladies at home in Sidcup and Chichester. My mother walks into the room. She is cross because our help has dressed me in my second best Shabbat outfit – a navy knitted skirt and jumper decorated with bunches of red knitted cherries and bleach-white socks. I know she'll make me change into last year's clothes, now designated as playing clothes. So we make our way back up the stairs, me begging to leave off the liberty bodice. But I'm aware that it's hopeless and first the liberty bodice and then the old tight clothes are forced over unwilling limbs. We come downstairs and I'm duly inspected.

'That's better,' she says. 'Good enough for playing in.'

I looked at her bright smiling face, eyes swollen from hours of crying – the colour masked with Pancake. I want to ask about the crying and the shouting, but somehow, even at four, I know not to. The rules are set. Tidy. Neat like my mother – the lady with standards. That's the way it was. She was a wife of the fifties and she never told. She lived in happy, happy land with her husband and her daughter and dedicated her life to perfecting their existence. That was what society demanded, and she would always obey. She was used to self-sacrifice.

But this story is not only about my mother. It could be your mother if she lived in the fifties, except she may not have had my mother's precarious start. No one who hasn't experienced life with an anorexic mother could imagine such a life. People might say that living with an alcoholic is similar and, yes, the relentless agony must be comparable. My family's tale is a chronicle of contrasts located in a convoluted world – of feasting and fasting. Slivers of joy slipped between chasms of sadness.

My parents' circumstances were not unique. There were many like my mother and my father: people who escaped from German oppression. My mother, Judith, came from Hamburg – the daughter of a religious and highly respected family – and in 1938 journeyed from there to the Hook of Holland and then to Harwich and finally to London. My father, Geoffrey, came from a small farming village outside Breslau. I do not know when or where he arrived. This story's beginning symbolises that time of separation, when young children were torn away from loving families, friends, a fluent language and secure lives, to cross a dangerous bridge to a hostile country, because of the onset of war. They were evacuated to families who took children into their homes, sometimes with altruistic motives, but often as a source of cheap labour. Moreover, these children were thrown into a society very different from their own, within a land of strangers. And this story does not stop with the survivors – the ones who 'made it', who adopted a new

3

country as theirs, absorbed their standards, became 'assimilated'. There is a second generation who are also suffering. In a way, this story is not about my parents but about me. There is so little told about the second generation. Sometime we mask our histories, afraid to tell. Some people, the extrovert personalities, are able to shout and sometimes bully their way through adversity under a defiant banner of pride – Yes We Are. So What! Maybe they are the survivors. But there are many more, such as myself, with more cloistered emotions, who still hurt and want to know why. There's a part of us that has never been allowed to leave the *shtetl* – that small Jewish village in Eastern Europe – and the ghetto. We witnessed and still live our parents' and relatives' pain in its many obscene forms, yet are expected to be tough: to cope. We stand in the wings as they perform their agonies on centre stage, watch, encourage, be comforter, sometimes nurse and even mother. We are the children of those who learnt that duty above all things is paramount. We learned German or Polish or Czechoslovakian, subliminally, through our skins as we took breath. The language of fear seeped into our blood, staining our understanding, our motivation, our confidence. But that language is part of the secret, not to be used, not to be spoken. It is packed away, locked in suitcases that wait on top of wardrobes to join the flight. The words of different lives. Not for others to hear. They must never know. They might suspect we are dissimilar. They might hate us for that.

This is the story of the second generation, but it starts, like all truths, at the beginning. So, 'Are you sitting comfortably? Then I'll begin.'

4

Chapter One

Are You Sitting Comfortably?

Before it all started. 1950, and I was four. I squatted on a leather pouffe – tan, imprinted with a star – hugging plump knees and, from the radio resting on the bookshelf, came a BBC lady's voice. 'Are you sitting comfortably?' she asked me, and as a dutiful child I replied, 'Yes.' Then, magically, without seeing me through the small mahogany frame and fine basket weave, but obviously hearing me, she said, 'Then I'll begin.'

So began my special time – those few minutes when the world circulated around me. A nursery rhyme, followed by a traditional story with a strong moral ending, usually about the exploits of princes, adventurous rabbits or children whose lives were very different from my own. Then another nursery rhyme, finishing with soft piano music. But for those brief minutes I floated from the morning room to enchanted palaces, to gardens that housed princesses, and swans that could speak, support four or five small children on their backs and, strong-winged, carry them to lands where people always smiled and shouting never happened. Then, when it was over, I was back in the morning room. Why the 'morning' room? It was decorated in beige embossed wallpaper with a border of orange and pinkish fruit and autumn-tone leaves. The paper was already on the walls when my parents moved into this Cardiff house, and they never changed it. On the far wall was a beige tiled fireplace that I knew my mother hated. She tried to bring out the pinkish colour by accenting it with a staggered row of pink

Ruth's fourth birthday

Sylvac rabbits. I was never allowed to play with them, even touch them, and I never disobeyed. The fireplace held a real fire that told stories in the flames and housed a secret city of goblins and elves – the fire fairies, immune to the burning temperatures – who watched us as we battled through our lives. Across the room from the fire was a small oak table, I suspect a junk-shop find, covered with a fresh seersucker cloth – the hand-embroidered cloths were saved for visitors – and four matching oak chairs with barley twist legs. I sat there with the mother's help, some terrifying female introduced into the house, supposedly to watch me and care for me.

I remember Betti – the first help of many to live across the landing next to my room. She was an elderly Welsh spinster with grey-wired hair and a single eye. She must have answered my mother's advertisement in the hope that she would idle away her final years with a family who wanted little besides some babysitting and ironing, and been more than satisfied with me, the perfect compliant only child. One night she stole food from the larder, a bread pudding and a bowl of custard cooling for a trifle, and blamed me for its disappearance. I tried to protest, but she stared at me with her single eye and terrified me. Another time she switched on the wireless and forgot to switch it off and my father heard the whispering sounds and furiously switched off the button, shouting about wasted electricity and was he Bloody Rockefeller? She said I was the culprit. As a result, she invoked an unknown devil within me, a side to my character that I had not known before. A sense of justice invaded my small body. I hated her. She was fair game. I hid her hair brushes, and loosened the top of her talcum powder, shaking a smoking cloud of Parma Violets into her underwear drawer.

The next Monday, I returned from the dentist with my mother, and Betti was gone. There was a note on the sideboard written in copperplate on scented violet paper saying how she'd never met such a despicable child and that she'd decided not to give her notice, but just to go. I felt my face redden with the injustice of it, and my tears flowed as I was accused of being the cause of her disappearance. And of shaming the family. I was to go to my bedroom and wait for my father to deal with me. I was terrified. My father was a large man – almost six feet – with an angry temperament and matching voice that would never listen to reason. It was impossible to placate his fury once he was roused. (To the outside world he presented a different picture. Strangers would see a smiling man, even-featured, who carried himself well and always looked good in clothes, with broad

7

shoulders tapering to wide wrists. He had thick wavy hair which fell softly over one eye if left in its natural state, but more often was slicked back into a smooth cap with an over-application of Brylcreem. His hands in some incongruous way seemed too small for his large build. They were small hands with manicured nails – a perfect white half-moon on each. He would spend every Sunday evening treating his nails. He used to mutter about people who had filth under their nails and how disgusting they were and he had special bowls for water and pots of cream. Only once my mother teased him about his nail attention, longing to escape the house and go out with him for a couple of hours. There were raised voices in their bedroom later.)

As I moved to my bedroom, my feet shuffled with fear over the polished brown lino. I seemed to sit on my bed for hours, swinging my legs, trying to think of songs that would divert my mind from my fate. But Mario Lanza was of little use. The slam of the door downstairs announced my father's return, and was followed by the muted sounds of my mother telling her story. My father shouted. I heard heavy footsteps and shook as his pounding feet ran up the thin-carpeted wooden stairs and drew closer with a sharp rat-tat of the lino outside my room. The heavy door swung open. He was white with anger. Words, angry consonants and vowels, formed with a bitter mouth, hurt more than the pain of the slap.

A few days later, my mother noticed that two of her favourite silver picture frames and a coffee pot had also disappeared.

Then, for a few weeks, it was bliss. My mother took sole charge of me. We did wonderful things together. Made pastry. My effort was rolled and re-rolled until it was grey and cut into shapes which stuck in the cutter but eventually made biscuits for my father to eat. I never saw him eat one. If he was home, which was rare, he'd wrinkle his nose and mutter, 'later'. Better were the stories we invented together, cutting pictures out of magazines to illustrate them. We had picnics in the park, and once we caught the train to 'Ponty'. It was the first time I'd seen bolts of cloth stacked, roll upon roll, a kaleidoscope of colour, and ducklings in cardboard boxes: peeping, tiny, fluffy creatures, ready to love. But it could not last. I knew that. Another gruesome woman would be employed to watch me. My mother returned to her small fashion concern, and I to the business of surviving the next harridan. But why so elderly? Why so sexless? Why so unpleasant? After all, my parents had to share a house with these females. It seemed to me, through my childish eyes, that these females were chosen specially by my mother for their ugliness, unsavoury armpits and hairiness.

The rules of the house insisted that, after breakfast, I was dispatched to the garden, unless it was raining heavily.

'Don't take your dolls out. You'll dirty them in the mud, and no…not your books…they'll spoil…You may have a ball… But don't throw it against the wall. Don't bang it!'

A ball for an only child when she wasn't allowed walls?

'And don't go out in the front. There are bad men lurking…they might steal you…they have…'

My imagination filled in the gaps. Giants with green teeth, putrid breath and glutinous fingers the colour and texture of slugs.

So I invented people in my green prison. I'd sit on the stone step leading from the kitchen door, hugging my knees and pulling my knitted skirt over the chubby bend of flesh to see how far the knit would stretch, conversing with my characters. Sometimes they were individuals remembered from radio stories, but chiefly they were half-people, nebulous morphs with the ability to change on demand, and with the predominant characteristics of my mother's friends. I would take the part of my mother. There would be invitations to send either by letter – smooth variegated ivy leaves were good for that – or phone, and then I would have to prepare the food for cocktails and intimate dinners.

9

'Victor, would you like to try these?' In my mind I'd made the tiny cream cheese boats I'd seen my mother prepare when she returned home from work. I'd watch her as she rubbed her back with the strain of it all. Nibbling all evening on a green pepper cut into slivers and three water-biscuits carefully laid out, as she prepared her elaborate banquets. In front of her would be trays of tiny tomatoes stuffed with tinned salmon mayonnaise, bite-sized vol-au-vents filled with mushrooms in wine sauce and bouchées – tiny mouth-sized morsels of choux-pastry filled with chopped anchovies and egg. Then she'd start on the frying – slivers of sole fried crisp, walnut-sized salmon rissoles to fit on the end of a cocktail stick, and lastly, slices of bread rolled flat smeared with butter and layered with cream cheese and chopped asparagus. They'd be cut into pin-wheels, kept fresh with a layer of damp tea cloths and arranged with all the other savouries. I would copy all these. The honeysuckle that hugged the stone wall between us and our neighbours was densely covered with glorious sticky red berries, lupines devoid of their hairy summer skins made wonderful substitute peas, and the discarded rhubarb fronds on the compost heap made plates.

Victor would always accept anything I cooked. 'You know how much I love your food,' he'd say, and then I'd turn to Lionel and say, 'Yes, darling, you are so sweet,' and I'd try the tinkling laugh.

If it rained, my life was easier because there was more to do indoors, except I was in the way of the Hoover, or the steaming-hot boiler bubbling on the kitchen stove, or the wooden muscles of a tyrant mangle that squashed my father's shirts to submission on clothes day and had been known to chomp a portion of finger. Usually, I was banned from the hysteria of the kitchen and settled alone in the morning room where I was allowed books and colouring and sometimes Plasticine. Though, whenever I used the last, there was always a row. No matter how careful I tried to be, a few miniscule blobs would find their way to the threadbare carpet to be squashed in by my Startrite soles. Sometimes the play with the Plasticine was worth the conflict, because time passed so quickly. The food for my people could be made to look realistic, and I could talk to my yellow and purple little bodies right up till lunch-time. And in the beginning, my mother came home from her fashion business to give me lunch. Perhaps only a small piece of 'yellow' haddock set next to smooth half globes of mashed potatoes, or two boiled eggs and a piece of bread, with the outline of a house complete with windows and a door, scraped out of a smear of butter. If I was ill she'd steam a small fillet of plaice in milk dotted with a little butter and there'd be pink semolina to follow – semolina cooked with a little milk, sugar and grated lemon rind and then coloured with a little pink colouring. But the type of food never mattered. It was that feeling of her, by my side: enveloping layers of softness and warmth. Tight cuddles with a slim body wrapped in an elegant suit, covered by a voluminous pinafore. A closeness and safety and a special time together.

But those days became less frequent as her business became more demanding. Mostly, on weekdays, I was left something on a covered plate for someone else to heat up and my mother really only existed as the highlight of my weekend. My father's presence too seemed to ebb, returning only in a violent wave of weekend presence.

But the drama of the Sabbath preparations began on the Thursday evening and sometimes I was allowed to stay up and watch, as my mother thought it was important for me to know how to kosher meat and to understand the Jewish laws and their logic. She'd return from work exhausted. Change into old clothes. Drink black coffees. Then take two white pills, smile brightly, rub some kind of cream over her aching shoulders, very occasionally smoke one Craven A, and begin the marathon. The meat that had arrived in brown paper parcels tied with string and smeared with blood had to be koshered. The parcels were unwrapped and grumbles and sighs followed.

'This roast he's sent – seems a bit small to me…! And the brisket's very fatty…I hope it's not going to be stringy …Thought I might get liver this week…oh well.'

It was laid out on a wooden board with slats so that when it was liberally doused with salt the excess blood would drain away. Then the meat was rinsed. An old boiling chicken would then be scalded and scraped. It was quite a dangerous process as this large bird would be immersed whole in boiling water, and my mother was a tiny woman. It took all her strength to remove the hot beast from the scalding liquid. While it was still hot, she would burn off (lovely smell) the remaining dark spines. The neck skin was saved to stuff with sausage meat, stitched with black cotton, and roasted for another meal. And the small chicken liver was burnt over the open flame of the gas so that it lost all its blood. It was then converted with the help of some fried onions, grated hard-boiled eggs, and a little of the rendered fat from the chicken, into chopped liver for the traditional starter and stored till the following evening. At that point I would be hastily dispatched to bed.

The Sabbath labours continued on Friday afternoon. She would rush in, tap-tapping her perfumed high-heeled dash I so adored. The table had to be laid with a snowy-white damask cloth, the best plates, the best glasses. My mother said that the Sabbath was a queen and we had to treat her as such. She would always manage to find two or three flowers from the garden, even in the midst of winter, to arrange in a small crystal vase to decorate the table. All the silver was polished. Not that my parents had much, but the few remnants of my mother's previous life, before her hasty exit from Germany – the candle-sticks of very thin silver plate, and a *becher* (a small silver beaker) – were given very loving treatment. Those were her precious pieces of another world: a world that would always make her cry. At that age I didn't understand why, as she sat rubbing, re-polishing and re-polishing, the tears would flow. We had someone in the house to help, but they were not allowed to touch these items. I assumed that silver religious articles were imbued with some magical but terrifying quality.

Once the table was laid my mother would start preparing the meal. There were only three of us (the help usually had the weekend off) and it was a marathon job, as food was prepared for the whole of the Sabbath and had to last until three stars could be seen in the sky on the Saturday night. But making vast amounts of food seemed to give her satisfaction. At that moment she was a creator. Her level of contentment was in proportion to her effort. However it was constantly assessed by some inner measure, the beating of an inner clock that surveyed her standards of perfection and constantly berated her endeavours. She could never make a half-hearted attempt. Everything had to be as perfect as she could manage. And in her eyes, it was never good enough.

She placed the chicken in a vast cooking pot with carrots, onions left whole, sticks of celery, and a good sprig of bay leaves, topped with water. It was simmered gently with the giblets until the flesh was almost slipping off the bones and the vegetables were meltingly soft. The cooked pieces were laid in a casserole with cooked rice and usually a rich mushroom and red wine sauce – she'd steal a little wine from Sabbath wine. We never drank any alcohol. (Not that there was any religious restriction on our alcohol intake.) This casserole would sit overnight in a very low oven to be served as our after-synagogue Sabbath feast. The liquor would be brought to the boil to remove excess fat which was lifted from the bubbling corner of the soup with a ladle.

'I wish I could do more on Thursday,' she'd sigh, readjusting her cotton peasant scarf tied over her head to protect the set waves.

'If only I had the time to do the chicken then, I could leave the soup overnight in the larder and just scrape the soft fat off the top.'

In the summer she would prepare mounds of potato salad to mix with chopped pickled cucumbers, and in the winter she'd make potato dumplings to a traditional German recipe. Half-cooked potatoes were grated and mixed with flour and dropped in boiling water to eat with the chicken. She always made gravy, thickly enriched with mushrooms, and cakes in case visitors arrived on the Sabbath. My father and I would eat our way through a vast chocolate-iced chocolate and vanilla marble cake which was cooked in the tin that was part of her past. That *gugelhupf* tin had been part of her small amount of luggage, brought as a memento of her home when she ran away from Germany – a little girl of twelve years old.

And still there was a *lockshen* pudding – the traditional Jewish dessert, noodles enriched with margarine, eggs and sugar, redolent with vanilla, lemon rind and juice and heavily solid with dried fruit. Sometimes there was an apple pie with apples out of the garden and a sugary crust and the juice running mixed with spices and sultanas. Yes, my mother could cook. She, I considered, was my Sabbath Queen.

We would wait for the sunset to pour gold over the apple trees at the bottom of the garden. I would have bathed and changed into my Sabbath best, and my mother would unfurl the voluminous apron, if she hadn't changed completely, and we would stand, calling my father many times until he appeared. He would have been resting. Earlier she had put out his slippers in welcome in the lounge, and had taken in a tray laid with a cloth she had embroidered herself, set with dishes of fresh home-made biscuits and his cup brimming with coffee. Then she would change out of her house-shoes and, slipping on the stilettos that she had discarded under the sideboard, resume her elegant stance.

14

'Quick,' she'd say. 'Quick, we must light the candles…
Shabbat is here.'

She'd cover her head with a small, black, Yemenite-
embroidered scarf that her English foster-mother had given
her, beckoning her arms in, close her eyes and say the
brochas – prayers to bring in the Sabbath.

Then it was my father's duty to say prayers over wine
and special *challa* bread dipped in a little salt. More often
than not he was reluctant to sing, and when he did, even
though he had what was then described as a perfect
crooner's voice, his stumbling or lack of enthusiasm would
prompt her. She was a bundle of impatience. She was ready
to sing, clear-voiced, songs she had learnt at her father's side
from the days when she shared his affection with her eight
siblings and her mother. With a voice flooded with emotion,
she would try to persuade my father to be part of her
invocation. Sometimes if he was 'in a good mood', he would
chant with her. But often, isolated and locked in a membrane
of recollection, she would raise teary eyes and sing to the
sky as if summoning her lost family and her god in a unique
solo.

Supper was usually encased in silence. Nothing would
be heard but the metallic chatter of cutlery on dishes.
Sometimes my mother would chop away at my father's body
of resentment with a pleading voice. Her desperation to talk
would be tossed away in exchange for a clipped answer. In
those days I did not understand my father's silent fury. How
he needed help. Nevertheless, chipping through the
atmosphere like the first-hatched noisy chick out of a brood,
my mother would try to teach me the Friday night songs. It
was only a matter of time before my father would become
angry, leave the table with a slam and take his food into the
lounge. Or worse, abandon his meal. I would see her follow
him with a plate, loaded with food.

'Geoff, Geoff, love…stay with us… It's Friday
night…please darling.' She'd run after him. Pull at his

clothes. This small woman – only five foot – dragging on the arm of a well-built six foot man. But he would always run away. It was his means of escape from a world he hated. When they were together, they always played this gruesome game. A kind of badminton. A to and fro of entreaty and anger. I was the shuttlecock, beaten between their racquets, losing feathers.

Her voice would float over the cream-carpeted horizon to the vacuum of a room I never saw as a child. I once saw his red moquette chair which I was aware housed his resentful persona. But the ending was always the same. I would be left with my mother, who would be fighting away tears, and forcing a smile. 'Darling,' she'd choke, turning to me, blinking and swallowing hard, rolling the edges of her Shabbat pinafore, 'your father's tired. He's had a hard week. You be extra good and go to sleep straight away.'

And I would manage to get into bed, hoping the devils would not be too troublesome when Daddy was so angry.

The Sabbath would continue like a large tired animal needing sleep. My father would have been away working (or, when he was home, keeping late hours) so he rarely accompanied us to the synagogue. In the early days, the synagogue was in the centre of Cardiff. A long walk for a young mother and baby. So we did not attend as often as we should. I understand now how terrible this lack of spiritual guidance and sustenance must have been for my mother. She was a deeply religious woman, whose father had been a Chief Rabbi, head of communities, uniting the cultural and spiritual desires of his flock with passion and love.

Sabbath moved gently into the afternoon. My father would take to his bed issuing noises of sleep through the walls, like an angry beast. My mother would try to joke with me at the sound, but nevertheless we would creep around the house for fear of waking him. I suspect it was for that reason, whenever the weather would permit, that we would walk. She loved to walk up the long steep hill, past the blocks of flats, to look at the grand houses. Her slim, elongated fingers with perfectly painted nails would point at the porches, conservatories, columns, or unusual windows. And always the gardens.

'Darling…look at that one…And that one…that one's got a bridge over a small stream…I bet they've got goldfish… One day we'll live in a house like that…With a real garden…and a swing and slide for you…and dozens of roses and white lilac trees and climbing wisteria…'

She had a way of pulling in her bottom lip with her teeth and clenching it. And screwing up her eyes with strong intention. I saw that so often when she was determined.

And while she was with me, I had her total attention. There was a summer moment, unusually hot, when a lorry loaded with boxes of grapefruit bounced over a bump in the road quite close to us. One very large pink grapefruit was thrown from an open crate in the lorry. It rolled, and landed in front of her. She tried to run after the driver to return it! But he was gone. We gazed at this treasure, unbelieving. Then she laughed and shrugged her shoulders. She tore the thick skin and the pith away, and the pink, sharp juice ran with our laughter. It was the first pink grapefruit I ever tasted. Later, she told me that the grapefruit had been sent from heaven and she believed this with a child-like resolution.

When autumn breathed rusty, crackling leaves about our heads, and threw more bundles about our feet clamouring to be kicked and chased, she'd note the location of blackberries for an afternoon's picking (no picking allowed on the Sabbath) or acorns and conkers and tell my father to drive there the next day, so she could collect them from the roadside and store these goodies for one of our rare play-times, creating animals with pins and creamy-white pipe-cleaners.

Despite her religious convictions, during these walks we would sometimes break the Jewish rule, the 'din', of not carrying. That was when our route would lead us to a doctor who would give her a prescription for the white pills. The ones that would make her run when she was tired. Allow her to make herself rise at four in the morning to prepare for a party, or brush her clothes ready for work, or ice one of my birthday cakes in the shape of a basket of teddy-bears, or a Disney Pluto. Anything that would prove her worth, and prove that she was a superwoman: able to run a home, a business, entertain, make clothes. The perfect wife.

I remember that birthday party. I have the photographs. Everything looks blissful. I'm a young child dressed in one of my mother's hand-smocked dresses that had taken hours of work to create, sitting in my father's best chair – the one with the dogs' heads carved on the arms. I'm blowing out my candles with my doting mother by my side. But the reality of that day is that I was banned to the garden so that she could finish preparing the finest food. There would be two separate tables. The children would sit in the garden on a long trestle table and the adults in comfort in the dining room. Many children would be invited, but none really that I could call my friend. Rather the children of my mother's friends. In fact some were children I secretly loathed, who pinched and were spiteful to me. And some were strangers. So there was an awkwardness, a discomfort, sitting amongst children I hardly knew or didn't want to know. I'm sure that parental choice of invitations to a child's party was the norm in every fifties house. The parents ruled and homes were run according to their wants and needs. Children's opinions were not considered. However, it was that uneasiness that must have prompted me to abandon the birthday table outside after the parents had moved on to their private tea, to sit happily in the quiet of the kitchen, eating the sandwich crusts, looking forward to home-time when all would leave and I could play with my new toys.

Winter months, when it was impossible to make the journey by foot for 'the pills-paper', she'd wait until dark,

18

after the Sabbath. Then we'd drive up to the grand house. And I'd wait with her in the doctor's dismal oak-panelled room. As he handed over the paper, I'd see her face change to happy. After, we'd come back to the house. She would disappear for a short while, then she might help me do some cork work with a cotton reel converted into a basic weaving instrument and we'd make dolly scarves; or we'd crochet or draw or even get the paints out. To welcome Chanukah into our home and show me that we could have celebrations as fine as gentiles with their Christmas trees, she'd crack walnuts and save perfect half shells. She'd scoop them out and we'd polish the shells with furniture wax. Then she'd fix small candles in them – candles left from my birthday, or small multi-coloured Chanukah candles – and she'd light them and float them in a large glass bowl. We'd turn out the lights, whispering and laughing and watch the magic boats carrying their glowing cargoes over the water. And I'd think of my fire fairies who would magically jump into the shells with their diaphanous golden wings spread in pleasure and the naughty goblins and elves, trying to overturn the tiny boats.

The coming of spring was a precious time in our house in those very early years. Even though she was busy, my mother would find the time to cut pussy willows and sticky buds from hedgerows with me and grow them in heavy jam-jars. We'd watch the sticky buds push off their insect-shiny, brown cases to show tiny green frills, and thick roots push into the glass jar bases. We'd start a hyacinth bulb in a special vase. Essentially though, spring signified the coming of the Passover to my mother. My mother relished that time, in contrast to most Jewish women, thoroughly enjoying the preparations – even the cleaning. The marathon cook-ins became even larger – on a vast scale, and with every morsel of food having to be home-made. My mother prepared at least eight types of biscuit, usually chocolate and vanilla pinwheels, cinnamon balls, coconut macaroons, almond macaroons, small biscuits dipped in chocolate, plus different flavoured meringues, three or four types of cake and pudding and numerous fish and meat dishes. Her friends would be invited to share in the feast. The table would be laid with a white cloth and a gold and white bone china tea-set she'd found in Woolworths, which was her best. On matching doily-covered plates she'd arrange matzos covered at the last minute (or they would go soggy) with chopped herring, egg and onion, and more dishes filled with dainty fish-balls. There would be hand-high sponges, pastries, and a chocolate cake made by soaking large matzos in coffee and layering them with a rich bitter chocolate cream sprinkled with toasted almonds. A centrepiece of daffodils with a few of the first sprigs of forsythia from the hedge would be arranged just before the visitors arrived. I'd see her face flushed and excited and I'd hear the compliments and for seconds she was important, fascinating and loved. My father, more often than not, would disappear as soon as he could, unable to cope with my mother's popularity. No one understood, except me, how long all these preparations had taken. For four weeks before, I heard her singing the old Hebrew songs from her childhood, wiping out shelves, re-tidying tidy cupboards late at night, making jams and lemon curd and pickles to sit on shelves in rows around the green and white kitchen. She would sit at the sewing machine creating a new outfit for herself for the synagogue, and I would have a mini version to match. I don't think she went to bed for those weeks. And she still worked in her office and gave me time.

During the long sandaled days of summer, in the very beginning, when the sun always seemed to shine, the weekends were devoted to the preparation of picnics. My sweetest memories are of these. I never knew how late my mother stayed up to make the perfect picnic. In the summer it was harder as the Sabbath would finish late in the evening; as a religious woman, she would only start her work after sunset. I sometimes saw a fish kettle-like pan with poached gefilte fish balls simmering gently on a liquid bed of carrots, onions, celery and a few bay leaves scrounged from a friend's garden. They were created out of a mixture of a few types of minced fish – traditionally, haddock, bream and cod – but every group of Jewish women followed a different custom, depending on their origins. The debate still continues about the perfect ingredients. I know my mother used raw egg, grated onions and herbs and plenty of salt, pepper and matzo-meal to make a fish dumpling that could be poached in a court bouillon or rolled in matzo meal and fried. These wonderful fish-balls were invented by the Jewish poor to extend a small amount of fish into a meal. My mother could make the most wonderful fishcakes out of a couple of tins of pink salmon and they would be equally as delicious. Then she would make her own mayonnaise, thick yellow and eggy-rich to accompany. Still not satisfied, she would make a pile of sandwiches and those were my favourite. With different breads, dark black, golden rye and creamy white, she'd make cucumber and cream cheese sandwiches, lettuce and sliced dill pickle, sardine and tomato (which in fact I hated as she insisted on leaving in the bones) and, finally, egg and cress. An egg sandwich is still my favourite food in the world. It tastes of childhood innocence and magic.

I realise now that the beach trips always involved other people. We arrived in Porthcawl – a small sea-side town twenty-five miles west of Cardiff – and made our way to Rest Bay, where we found rows of my parents' friends spread out in long extended semi-circles. The area would be a patchwork of windbreaks and rugs on the sand and baskets with Thermos flasks sticking out like metal rockets from rolls of towels and stacks of spare deck chairs tucked into rocks. After the car was unloaded and everything was brought down into a pile of 'essentials', my mother would sit on a rug on her knees, toe-nails painted red to match the fingers and lips, and her polished golden skin making her look like a blonde goddess. She'd be dressed in her newly-made bathing suit and played her audience as she unpacked her goodies. Each basket had been carefully embellished over months with red and white gingham and matching serviettes. She'd hear the words of approbation and she would glow. She wanted to achieve perfection and that was her way. She was driven. She always made triple the amount of food we needed so everybody could eat some of ours. The menu had to be more elaborate than other people's, with a Kilner jar full of potato salad, small savoury tarts, an apple pie or a cake heavy with fruit, or tiny fairy cakes with thick lemon icing, and always jelly and blancmange – red and pink mixed in more vast Kilner jars. Of course my father always provoked at least one row in front of everyone – either over the amount of food he had to carry, or the distance he had to walk with deck-chairs and accessories. Nevertheless I loved those days – especially my moments in the sea with the waves trying to pull me over and play with me, twisting their salty muscles. I was always lost when I came out and imagined that everyone had decamped and left me, but I never panicked and, feeling the slap of a knitted bathing costume about my thighs, I'd chase back up to the groups of people with the stiff Porthcawl wind battering my hair, and the hard dampness of gritty sand numbing my feet, till I came to the soft velvety warmth, hoping that someone would recognise me and that there would be a dry warm towel, a drink and a left-over piece of pie. And strangely enough, I always managed to find our group.

Conversely, I hated the way home. By then my father would be shouting in the car, driving too fast as if the car was a horse he had to force to go faster. I was usually car-sick. But the image of my mother on the beach – happy, enjoying, contented – is how I like to remember her.

Chapter Two

Everything Changes

Then, one summer's day in 1951, when I was five, my mother disappeared. There was no explanation. Without warning, the radio was silent, and the vases sat about the house holding withered stalks and dank brown water. Visitors and their laughter were no more, my mother's magical cooking scents were absent, my privileged time in the morning room when the lady spoke to me on the radio had gone, and, over the weeks, Shabbat became just a sweet memory. Now, the witches and the monsters ruled supreme in my bedroom, taking over the coat peg in the darkness and scratching and sharpening their claws under my bed. There was a lady in the house, one of the usual helps who watched me, but I was so distraught that whatever she said meant nothing. My father seemed to be around the house more, that is to say, I heard his shouts. In September the help left, and I began school.

My mother's disappearance seemed to last forever. But in fact it was for about a month. At last she came home, oh joy! A wonderful surprise – no one had told me she was returning. But everything had changed. My mother seemed to live upstairs. Downstairs and its importance faded. It had become what it always must have been, a lonely grouping of second-hand furniture in a tired, neglected arrangement of bricks and mortar. On the first day of her return I was allowed to see her for a few minutes. I tried to jump on her bed to play but was pulled off and told that I could whisper from the door to a body in a bed swathed in bandages. She turned her head and tried to smile at me and then turned away from me and began sobbing, as if my reality was too painful. She didn't seem to want to talk to me and, after that, she lay for hours on her own, in her room. There was one occasion when I thought I might see her properly. I crept up the stairs and into the sleeping darkness of her room and climbed on to the bed. I wanted her to be my mummy again. I needed to get close and squeeze and have hugs with her like we had in the past. But her whole body juddered as I moved next to her. Her voice was strained. In the curtained gloom, I could just see that her breasts were tightly bound with heavy bandages. (She told me later that she had *stones* in her breasts. I suspect they were some kind of tumor – I was never allowed to ask questions.) She smelt of Dettol and antiseptic and she pushed me away.

'Darling, you're hurting me,' she gasped. 'Please get off!'

Then my father heard us and I was whisked away. No one told me what the bandages meant or why she didn't want my love any more. Their bedroom was out of bounds and I noticed that my father more often than not slept in the spare bedroom. Our lives had changed forever.

I'm sure she realised that I had been neglected and wanted to comfort me because it was then she persuaded my father to buy me a puppy. Whiskey arrived on a sunny day. She was a golden cocker spaniel with long silky ears and long eyelashes that covered dark eyes – pools of love. I adored her and dressed her in my dolls' clothes, pushing her around the garden in the dolls' pram. I felt at last I had a real friend. Someone to talk to and love. But she was bought in the usual manner – in haste, with little care. She was highly strung and over-bred and puddled everywhere. Of course, puppies puddle and are destructive. And spaniels can be particularly neurotic. I ran home one day looking forward to playing with Whiskey but couldn't find her.

'She's gone,' said one of the harridans who helped my mother.

'Where?' I asked.

'She's gone away to a farm where she can't do so much damage. And good riddance too – damned nuisance, always piddling on my clean floors!'

I sat in the garden clutching one of my dolls, rocking back and fore and crying. I vowed that when I was a big girl I would have a doggie. No one ever sat with me and talked about the loss of the dog. That was one of the most difficult moments of my childhood.

And now my mother, although no longer bed-ridden, seemed to be even more detached. There were absences. Weeks when she disappeared. Her friends would make a show of taking me out for a meal or buy me a bag of sweets as a comforter. I wanted to ask my father. I must have questioned. I must have wanted to ask, but he never talked to me about my mother's absence Now, years later, I can only assume that my mother was not only suffering physically from the pain of that operation but, worse, from a form of depression. Certainly, the wide, purple scars that mutilated her small but beautiful breasts, extending under each breast, and then to the centre of each, to the nipple, must have caused her excruciating pain and damaged her view of herself as a beautiful, sexual person. All I know is that from that time nothing was the same again.

I did notice, though, during that time of illness, that Geoffrey was a different man with my mother. He was loving, considerate, charming. People came to the house to visit her and he would be the entertainer.

'It must be such fun to have a father like Geoffrey,' they laughed. 'He's so full of jokes and fun…the life and soul of the party.'

I didn't know this man. But I was glad to see him that way. To my mother he must have suddenly become the lover he had once been. While she was ill and swathed immobile in bandages, he would walk in with armfuls of flowers, a piece of elegant nightwear, an extravagant box of chocolates. She would respond with delight, naturally, but at the same time there was an undercurrent of intense emotion in the air as if we all lived in a pressure cooker and the thing could explode at any minute.

Of course my mother enjoyed my father's sudden attentions. It was as if the workings of humankind had stopped, for them, for a while. After all, they had originally met in a sickroom. They were two young Jewish evacuees living in a cheap London boarding-house trying to make a life, and at that time, 1943, my mother was temporarily relieved from her work driving a hose-laying lorry in the fire-service, and was upstairs in bed, sick. He heard that she was ill and took her a cup of tea. So it was Hitler who brought my parents together. But it was Hitler who also helped to destroy them. Many others were successful in their cultural transplant, but after her first illness and the resurgence of my father's attention, my mother remained ill. My father relinquished his pattern-cutting job in a factory, and began running my mother's small business of selling a few fashions from a small room. She no longer picked me up from school and stayed away in nursing homes or small hotels by the beach, to recuperate. I know now that there was far more going on than I realised at the time. But I was small. And explanations were not given to children in the fifties.

By now there were no live-in ladies to care for me, and I was attending infant's school full-time. While my mother was away for weeks at a time, searching for something to pacify her internal pain, the pungent smell of smoke grew within my life. My father had always smoked cigarettes. Now the stench of smoke would announce his appearance when I was bathing. He would push open the door and insist on scrubbing me and his invasive hands hurt me and I wanted him to stop. Sometimes, when I was in bed, a knife of light would blade the base of my bedroom door. I would hear his feet outside and my heart would start to bang in my chest. He would open the door and stand in the doorway dressed only in his underwear, and I would feel trapped in my darkness. Then he would walk into my room with the red core of a cigarette in his hand. I would see him and the outline of his maleness in his thin underwear through squeezed eyes and pretend I was asleep. He would lean over the bed and whisper, 'Are you awake?' I would close my eyes even tighter and he would leave. In my bedroom, it was a staring thing, not like the touching in the bath. But I was always afraid. That silhouette in the doorway and the smell of the smoke was terrifying. I hated his moods and didn't know why he stared at me so intently. Luckily, that phase did not last very long – I suspect because he realised I was close to my mother and maybe in the future would reveal the story of the evening bath-times. But to this day I hate the smell of smoke and cannot sleep with the odorous reek about my body. One night after a good party, my husband found me in the bath scrubbing away the stink with tears welling in my eyes.

'What's the matter, love?' he whispered. 'I thought we had a brilliant time.' I managed to explain a little but, as I stumbled with the words, I felt soiled and ashamed. I've buried these facts until now. They've lived under my feet, tripping my confidence, making me feel inadequate. But in order to look at the fate of the second generation, it is vital to lift all the sealed stones laid on the path of respectability. It explains to me why, even at a very young age, I felt pinned with the badge of 'victim'.

School gave no comfort. Is it so long ago, just during the fifties, that we stayed silent to teachers and parents? Parents were unaware of their children's unhappiness and as pupils we never spoke of our distress. We drank our warmish milk from small glass bottles, and hated it. The outside concrete sheds they called toilets were places of horror where the older bully-boys and the spiders ruled. Lessons were formal – rote and recitation – and apart from making paper chains to festoon the walls at Christmas, it was a joyless place. When I returned home, I had to endure my father's cooking which might consist of boiling a large piece of shin of beef in water with unpeeled vegetables until the lot went brown. We ate chunks of the glutinous meat in the fetid water, dipping in hunks of soured brown bread. Even that was a better option than lights, yes, lungs, boiled in a saucepan. As they cooked they swelled up as if breathing, sometimes, monster-like, pushing the saucepan lid out of the way. When they were cut they revealed the white bronchial alleys. We even found a windpipe once, though fortunately that was cut out and discarded. My father was trying his best. He was managing the care of a small child whilst trying to work. No one felt they should help, or maybe he refused offers. He had a dogmatic insistence that he knew everything. He thought that comfort in the shape of a shoe box of sweets (I have always hated chocolates) was the best panacea for a lonely child and, apparently, after one particularly long trip when my mother sought refuge in a sanatorium in Israel, she returned to find a fat child bursting out of her seams, instead of the slim five-year old she had left in his charge.

While she was still away, and without explanation from my father, I found myself picked up by a stranger after kindergarten who took me to her home. I was expected to spend my free hours with her and her family. I didn't know who she was. She was never introduced to me. I used to stand in the cloakroom outside the classroom and this woman would call for me. The teacher would hand her a small bag of food for my lunch, a toy maybe, and a change of knickers – in case. Then, suddenly – it must have been the school holidays – I had to stay during the day with her and her family. I hated everything about that place: her husband lounging in his underwear in the sitting room/kitchen, the rough exchanges of abusive words and occasional raucous laughter between the family coupled with the sour unwashed smell of those strangers. Years later I smelt that odour again and felt the prickle of fear spike my body, when I visited a family as a charity worker. For weeks the origins of that scent eluded me. Now I would call it neglect. A milk bottle always stood on the table laid with newspaper, with its contents set in a sour ring. Next to it would be a folded bag of sugar, in contrast to my mother's pristine sugar basin, a bottle of tomato ketchup (I've always hated that stuff) and, on a grimy stove, a chip-pan at the ready set with greyish-yellow dripping. There was a shut-tight smell of damp combined with a drying clothes-horse and unwashed body odour. I didn't know or understand these people. And the most hated part of this experience was the young son – Leslie – who was expected to be my companion. Or at least keep me quiet and removed from sight. He was years older than me and I was a nuisance to him. I couldn't even ride a bike. So the only way to manage his new charge was to lock me in the cupboard under the stairs. I cried to my father, pleading with him to let me stay at home, but he never listened. Occasionally, at this time, my mother reappeared in the house, but seemed preoccupied. Not hearing, as if other worlds or voices were speaking to her. And my father started to be at home more; that is to say, I heard his shouts with increased frequency. But no one really talked to me and life seemed filled with unresolved fears.

Finally, the woman lost my home-prepared cheese sandwich out of the bag on the way home and served me a sausage fry-up when she cooked her family's lunch. I looked down at my plate. I was a good girl and always ate up my food. But I knew something was wrong. I tried to eat it to please her, but there was a taste of fat and I only had a little. Just before I left, Mrs Skinning caught my arm. It hurt as she pulled.

'You dare tell your Dad that you had sausages and I'll tell 'em that you were a bad girl.'

I hadn't done anything. I hadn't even cried when Leslie locked me in the cupboard. By the time I arrived home I was feeling extremely sick. My mother was home at the time and concerned for me. She asked what else I'd eaten that day.

'I can't tell you,' I said. 'I'll have a row from Mrs Skinning.'

'But why should you have a row from her? Have you done something very naughty?'

'No. But…'

'But what, love? Tell me.'

And so it all came out: the threat and the cupboard under the stairs, but most of all, the sausage fry-up. I never went to Mrs Skinning's house again. I stayed with a neighbour and a child of a similar age and that was better.

It was about two years later that my mother returned on a more permanent basis from her hospitals and sanatoria. The house was filled with a warm glow, the night visits finished and I was safe. *Music While You Work* played in our house again. My mother returned to the marathon cooking sessions each week and on a Sunday the British Forces Network in Germany asked for requests. But I never felt secure again. It seemed as if though the wounds on her body were healing – she even tried to go back to work a little – she was carrying scars larger than the physical. She was now a fragile woman, haunted by unrelenting ghosts. There would be a letter on the radio, a documentary about the war or someone requesting a German marching song, and my mother would scream, sometimes putting her hands to her face in terror. Within hours she would be ill, sometimes moving back to her bed or even out of the house, for weeks, and I would again be left lonely in school and home.

It was about that time that I learnt the language of compliancy. That it was better to do as asked, and find solace in my own imagination. I never argued, for to disagree was to incur my father's anger. There was one particular party at one of the Jewish girls' houses. My mother was absent. The invitation fell through the door and I was thrilled. I was never close to any of them but I yearned to be part of that life – that enclosed circle. I knew all the girls I had watched at the synagogue, and spoken to occasionally, would be there and I had to have a new dress. With my extra poundage and growing height, it meant that my old dress was far too small. Approaching my father after he had worked in the day – getting past the height of the newspaper – was never easy. He sat in the lounge with the radiogram banging out the boom of Beethoven and I pushed open the door.

'Yes, Ruth,' he barked, 'what do you want now? The supper will be a while, take some bread if you're hungry.'

'I was wondering if I could have a new dress. It's Beccy's party and everybody's going.'

'It's always everybody – every bloody body!'

'I would like to go but my dress doesn't fit.'

'So what makes it so important to go with that bunch of spoiled brats?'

'They are the only people I know apart from those in school. Please can I go?'

I should have left the whole idea sealed in its envelope. My father asked a neighbour to take me after school to buy a suitable dress. Fearful of his outbursts but having some fondness for me, this lady took me into town. Clothes for overweight children were hard to buy in the fifties. Party dresses were elaborate affairs and usually very expensive. My escort was afraid of my father's temper and looked for the cheapest. We left the shop with a garment made in a rayon-type fabric with blue and silver wide horizontal stripes and sparkling buttons which pulled against my pre-pubertal breast. I remember saying to her, 'I've only got my Startrite brown lace-ups,' but my words fell on the concrete stones. I loved the sparkly buttons but knew even then that the dress enlarged my shape, so I sat in my room and I ate a packet of biscuits and a tube of spangles. Later I tried to ask him: *Please could I have a pair of shoes* – that at least would have made the horizontal stripes a little less evident, especially as the dress did have a wonderful swishyness. But he growled like a bear.

'You've got your bloody dress and you'll wear it with your new lace-ups and be grateful. You can look at yourself in your mother's mirror as a treat.' He disapproved of mirrors. But that only made the situation worse. I was perhaps seven or maybe just eight but I can remember looking at my shiny bursting reflection, with white socks sinking into polished tight brown lace-ups, and knowing that I looked utterly ridiculous.

Outside the house there were balloons swirling in the wind and I walked up the drive clutching a wrapped book which my father had purchased in anger at the final moment. I rang the bell and could hear peals of laughter from the other side of the glass door. The party had already started. Groups of girls in diaphanous slim dresses all ran to the door, some wearing real stockings and party shoes, silver and black patent, and my dream – bunny-wool boleros. I hadn't even bothered to ask about those. I stood in the hall and removed my navy school mac and walked very slowly into the lounge which was decorated with more balloons.

One little girl who was the spoilt baby in a family of very rich indulged children walked up to me.

'Is that your party outfit, Roofi Poofi?'

The others, yearning to be in her gang, joined hands and danced around me shouting 'Roofi Poofi!' With my ability to fight back destroyed by my father, I just absorbed their cruelties like a sponge. From that moment I hated parties. They continued their taunting until almost time to go home. The mothers were happily ensconced in another room enjoying a rare glass of sherry and tea and sandwiches, happy that the children seemed to be playing so nicely.

So I returned to my bedroom, imagination, books and my shoe box of sweets. A quiet and compliant child incurred less trouble. However, in my mind rested a dormant animal, learning, observing and knowing that one day I would break free from the tyrannies of my home and outside. But it was to be a long, painful journey.

And, in the meantime, the temper of school life and home showed little improvement. In school, Fatty was an easy target for jokes that speared and hurt me. I was never provided with the ammunition to retaliate and for this the teachers were as much to blame as the pupils. But life progressed, and despite my ever-increasing size, bolstered by a steady diet of sweets, biscuits, and, when my mother was well enough to cook, marathon feed-ups, I remained outwardly a happy person. 'She's so good – such an easy child – never a second's problems with her.'

Yes, 'good', that was easier, yes, compliant. That kept me safe.

My mother, when home and not in a sanatorium, was as vulnerable as a tightrope walker, balanced only by the artificial crutch of her magic tablets. I discovered later that they were amphetamines It was becoming increasingly difficult for her to walk for her prescriptions. So the obliging doctor now called and left the crisp white private prescription lying at the side of the bed in return for cash. It was my job to get the prescription filled. Once a pharmacist asked me why my mother was taking so many of these drugs.

I stood in his pharmacy as he bent down to me.

'You know your dear mother shouldn't need so much of these.' When I returned home, I innocently described the discussion to my parents. It was as if I had broken some religious commandment. My mother sobbed and my father screamed. Then he picked up the phone and bawled at the pharmacist.

Much later, during a trip to London to see another doctor and without my father, (I must have been eleven) my mother sent me to Piccadilly on my own to pick up a prescription and I walked through Paddington and Soho terrified. I never questioned her motives. I'm sure she didn't realise how dangerous that walk was, for she loved me and would never hurt me. But her innocence of the outside world plus the power of that piece of paper transcended all judgements.

For the coronation of Queen Elizabeth, in 1953, my mother made a special cake in the shape of a crown. It took her two days. The base was thin short-crust pastry baked in a large circle. Tiny choux puffs filled with cream and confectioner's custard were arranged around the edge and the centre filled with more custard. Then the cake was studded with soft fruit, raspberries and dessert gooseberries and red-currants, to look like jewels. On the day, friends and neighbours squashed into the lounge to watch the new television specially purchased for the occasion. Photographs were taken. The Coronation cake was demolished and was voted the best-flavoured, most tempting and the most exquisite of all cakes.

Mum always needed the big project — something that would hook in her imagination like a muscular fish fighting on a taut line. She would need an all-involving mission – a scheme – sometimes too large for her but something that totally engaged her imagination and left no space for the bad. Now, she began to draw up plans for a house. She worked with an architect for hours, wearing a crisp oversized white shirt and tight, tiny, black matador trousers to emphasise her slimness, sitting over vast sheaves of drawings that hung over the dining-room table. She was going to build her house up the hill, to her own design. It was the house she dreamt of. The one with the large garden for me planted with roses and a small winding path in the front and a gate surrounded by more rose hedges.

We took an expedition up the hill. I ran around a large field up to my waist in whispering grasses, unaware that this would be the plot of land designated as our future home. Growing alongside those tickling stems were thicker stalks heavy with clusters of white bells. I picked an armful of the white bluebells and didn't notice a glutinous slime oozing from the stem ends. Running back to my parents I called, 'Mummy, Mummy, look, I've picked you both a present.' I knew how much my mother adored cut flowers. They both screamed in unison.

'You stink! What have you been picking…? Now we'll have to change your clothes and there's nowhere to wash you here.' That was my first experience of wild garlic.

With the purchase of the plot of land, our financial commitments changed and also my parents' relationship. My father would have to work harder, which would send him away for longer periods of time. Neither of them anticipated that. My mother was absorbed by her dream, and he was going to prove to the world, I think, that he was a successful businessman. It all seemed such a fantastic, unrealistic, conception. And it marked the moment when my mother changed forever into 'The Sick Woman'.

Judith in the 'dream house' garden

Chapter Three

Moving to the Prison

We moved to Bryngwyn Road, Cyncoed, in the summer of 1957. I was eleven. For its time, the house was extraordinary. I think my mother yearned to be the next Frank Lloyd Wright. It was an arrangement of connecting boxes, with a magical flow of interior space. Two very large rooms downstairs, the dream kitchen decorated in pale blue with the latest Formica, and a breakfast bar in one corner, like a small American diner, fitted with red imitation buttoned leather. The kitchen curved through a small dining area – hardly used – into a vast lounge laid with cork tiles and polished to a slippery gleam, with a stone wall that ran the length of the room, containing holes – a fireplace, a space for logs, and niches for ornaments. And on the opposite side, floor-length Venetian blinds – the bane of my life, for it was often my job to dust these mini knives that sliced hands and fingers with deadly accuracy. And there was a crazy fifties touch – a cream wall buttoned with imitation leather cladding the side of the staircase. The new home should have been the focus for an ideal life, a beautiful place.

But Mum became sicker. As an eleven year old I knew nothing specific about her illness. Her condition was still veiled in secrecy and I was in school all day. I didn't question how she lost weight. I just never saw her eat with us. She used to dish out food to my father and myself and not eat but we never asked why. She always told me that she had eaten in work (when she was able to go to her fashion showroom) and that she'd just like a couple of high-baked crackers and a thin slice of Edam cheese, with masses of green pepper. I knew she took laxatives – dozens a day, all types. I was an expert on the makes of laxatives available, from chocolate to tiny pills, and powdered herbs that made her gag as she tried to swallow them. And of course, she was frequently sick. But as a child I never connected her loss of weight to an illness. Her bizarre behaviour seemed normal because I had so little experience of anything else.

This sense of normality was shaken, however, when, just after we moved, we took a cruise. The idea must have been to allow my parents to relax – a brief escape from all their anxieties. But the reality was hideous. Once we embarked our problems as a family escalated. We shared two small cabins in the cheapest part of the ship with only one porthole which I suspect was false and placed merely to give an impression of a window. Because of my father's snoring – at least that was the excuse I was offered at the time – I moved in with my mother, my father taking the single. I was trapped. When we did venture out on to one of the floors, we were besieged by the staring eyes of people who had never seen someone as ill as my mother before. Her parchment skin was white. Thin lips dragged over teeth that now seemed too large, and black shadows carved deep sockets around her sad eyes. Sadness was so much part of her persona that she looked like a rescue dog locked in a kennel. Her arms were as thin as other people's wrists and the skin about them fell in pleats. She constantly worried about the eyes and pointed fingers.

'That woman's gawping at me, Geoffrey. Do something about it. Stop her...tell her off!'

My father was embarrassed. He no longer enjoyed his role of lover to a sick woman and urged my mother to ignore the rudeness though making sure the offender could hear. This became a daily event, sometimes more often, until eventually my mother retreated and hardly emerged from her cabin. I felt constantly shamed and was grateful when she finally hid from others. From then I spent most of my time carrying trays down to the bowels of a juddering ship. We returned to our new home with poor Mum a sicker person at the end of the holiday than at its beginning.

Judith & Ruth during cruise holiday

The consequence of that exposure was to last forever. The pattern of starvation my mother adopted in that muttering, swaying, ship stayed with her for the rest of her life. Someone would be cruel. She would eat as a kind of comfort, and then, as if the food was a lump of bitterness that had to be exhumed, she would bang her flat-boned rib-cage and belly until all the food was removed. On that cruise, our tiny shared cell reeked of vomit. Then she would purge her body with laxatives to remove the final tiny scraps.

On that cruise too, my father learnt to escape. The other blueprint of our life. From then, when the going got tough, my father was gone. And I kept the secret. For years no one knew that my father became almost a stranger in our house. At eleven years of age I assumed the role of carer, nurse, cook and companion. I never minded. I loved my mother and longed to see her better, living with the silly delusion that one day everything would be better, and our lives would be as they had been when I was five.

From our return, it was as if a large animal had swallowed my previous life. In the old house, I had been a plumpish child whose mother had bouts of sickness, but who for some of the time was 'normal'. We sat at the table together occasionally, shared a few meals, went on picnics, a few trips in the car. And I attended a school that was bearable, comforting, safe. I heard laughter, albeit rarely. But now it was as if a hydra of the first life, still in the previous world's skin, had sucked up the past and replaced it with a festering sack of ghosts and recriminations. There was a framed Hieronymus Bosch picture along the corridor of my new school showing the sufferers in hell with parts of their body eaten away by red fiends. I used to stare at this picture and think that hell was not that far away.

At home, inside, when the doors were shut, we played those new roles created by the demons that ate both my parents. Every day we were reminded of the past. My parents still used German to talk between themselves. Their roles in that life were still being acted out. They were still prisoners of Adolf Hitler. We never talked about our beginnings. We lived in fear that someone might, 'G-d forbid shveig, shveig,' discover that we had German origins. My mother only had to hear a German lullaby or see a Nazi flag to become upset and yet it was my father's hobby to watch war films on the television. Eventually, Mum would beg him to stop, and as usual he would take offence and disappear. She lived with the fear that someone would take her remaining family away and her anxieties were compounded each time my father walked out of the house. And to aggravate the situation further, we were surrounded by strangers, now we had moved to the dream house on the hill. Next door's closeness had gone. We knew none of the neighbours and, if anyone did call, my father always presumed that they were being nosy or interfering and would shout at them to go away. They never returned.

Every one of my days ran its ugly course with claustrophobic insistence, only changing if my mother's health became worse. I considered myself lucky if it was school-time and my mother had not been too ill the night before, because then I would have managed some of my homework and could leave the house, even if it was at the last minute, squeezing in some jobs before I left. I would be chasing around with my uniform just pressed and satchel to the ready, and my mother would need a full bed-pan emptied. Or I might have to set a tray ready for her – or fill a thermos flask, empty a sick-bowl. In readiness for the Sabbath, usually on a Wednesday, I would have to order the food which was delivered to the house in various vans, and then there were my father's shirts that had to be checked for the laundry, my mother's bed to be remade, her pillows to be plumped – anything, it seemed to me, to delay my departure. At last, my father would drive me to school. Some would say that I was lucky to have a lift, but in fact I would have preferred the bus. The chance to be with others, for even a few minutes, was something I craved. An utter bloody loneliness shrieked through my days. On the very odd occasion when I did manage to catch the bus I enjoyed eavesdropping on the banter or sitting on one of the side seats downstairs and just being with people who demanded nothing from me and sometimes offered me a smile.

In this grammar school, the 'firsties' were fair bait, especially the fat ones, and 5C, who enjoyed a laugh, 'initiated' me by grabbing the very expensive pristine, uniform beret, pulling out the top twist of felt and shoving the beret in the mud. Trying to join in the laughter, I retrieved it – now sporting a large hole in the centre and plastered with mud. I stuffed its stinking squelchyness at the bottom of my satchel. But the next morning my father questioned its disappearance. I was made to show him. After that time, discomfort hung around my desk, and told me that nowhere was safe. So I pretended that everything was fine.

But school was always a problem. I didn't fit the mould. Apart from the times when my mother was sick, I took time off for religious days (although I very rarely attended the synagogue once my mother became too ill to be left). So there were gaps in my education. The effect was cumulative. Those High Holidays, a month of feasting and fasting, wreaked great damage. They would fall on the same two days for four consecutive weeks at the beginning of the new school year. Inevitably this would clash with a difficult subject – Latin, physics or double maths. Missing the beginning meant that numbers would remain an unknown clouded in the mists of pi and isosceles. Whilst the rest of my class were unfathoming the mysteries of long division and multiplication, I was walking to the synagogue in my best and saying blessings for a good sweet year.

One year, when I returned, I approached a teacher whose classes I had missed.

'Please,' I whispered. 'Could I have the notes of…?'

My voice faltered as I looked at her grey folded face. Mouth set tight into a letter-box and eyes watery-blue as if the colour had been washed away. She lowered her head to stare at me.

'Yes?' Those eyes glittered back at me.

'Do you think…I could have the …'

'You make your own arrangements.' She rubbed a tense shoulder muscle. Then hissed in a strong Irish accent, 'You Christ killers take everything.'

I was just twelve years old, but even now I don't understand what she meant. On that day I felt more separate than at any time before, or since. I choked away the tears. To exacerbate the situation it was lunch-time and it was the rule that I ate my kosher food on a table away from the others, separated and defined as 'a sandwich girl'. No wonder food began to assume an ugly persona. It insinuated isolation, annihilation. I said nothing later to my father who would have thrown a tantrum in the headmistress's office.

As other girls reached their teens, wore jeans, make-up, and high heels, my mother decided that I should wear a corset. I'm sure she had good intentions, but in effect the binding formed an entrapment like the binding of a traditional Chinese woman's feet. And the mocking, staring agonies in the changing rooms and showers in school would stay with me forever. She made this decision when I was twelve years old and fully developed. My mother could still drive then when 'well', and she took me to a ladies' underwear shop to get a 'foundation' made. It was the fashion for older woman at that time. We walked into a badly-lit shadowy room that stank of stale perfume. Two women of indeterminate age dressed in knitted suits and pearl necklaces moved toward us with tape measures and told me to undress completely except for my panties. I felt uncomfortable; I didn't want to expose my secret flesh to strangers. There was weirdness about these women scrutinising my body. I hated them touching my breasts with their tape-measures. I loathed their stray fingers and wanted to escape. I felt as if I was suffocating. At last we could leave. I'd had 'the fitting'. I dreaded our return but could not think of a sensible excuse. My mother told me that wearing a correct foundation was part of becoming a woman. Later, when the garments were ready, they forced my body into so-called flesh-coloured orange elastic-and-wire deep bras with a row of unyielding hooks and eyes. I wanted to breathe large gasps of air. Then they laced and hooked me into a corset that was supposed to meet the bra to form a perfect whole. They pulled at my breasts with my mother watching, and tweaked the fit until I felt sick. And when I was encased in their steel and elastic creation, they gazed at me with satisfaction. I needed to leave. I wanted to cry but I had to be pleased. To thank my mother for her kindness, carry home the spares and wear those hateful encumbrances.

At night, I peeled off their garments. My body was covered with weals where the edges had rubbed during the day. From then on, every night, I would find open wounds around my waist and under my breasts where spare pieces of flesh had been caught in the corset and formed a tight red blister. I'd slide into the bath; the sting was agony. The following days I would layer the gaps with pieces of cotton wool and tissues to prevent the irritatation but my temporary corset bandages usually fell out as I walked and compounded my embarrassment. Being made to wear those corsets was one of the greatest cruelties of being a big girl. And my mother, who loved me, still called me her 'Fattus Palinsky', as a term of endearment.

But I felt a huge and horrible responsibility for her. Slowly but definitely, as my mother's sickness worsened, my father's appearances decreased. The illness seemed to be related to my father's attention. When we were in crisis, as her screams of anguish rent the open-plan emptiness, away from her eyes I'd pray for her to get better or for someone to help me, and he would suddenly return and show his love (or whatever he would have called it) with bought things: flowers and exotic fruit, and, later, when the crises worsened, pieces of jewellery.

They were only repeating the pattern of their beginning.

Chapter Four

Their Stories

My mother and father met in a Jewish boarding house in 1943 when they were both attempting to rebuild two dreadfully damaged lives. My mother had arrived in Britain late in 1938 at the age of twelve with her older brother, after saying goodbye to a close, devoted, respected family. Her father was the Chief Rabbi of Hamburg, and there were nine children plus numerous uncles, aunts, cousins and friends. She had never been parted from them before. She must have watched her family make the last-minute preparations for her journey, packing special items in a small suitcase: a pair of thin silver candlesticks, a gugelhopf cake tin; small reminders of a solid safe life that was to be shattered forever. (As a mother and grandmother, I can only imagine the terror – the sheer bloody sick yellow fear.) The parents would have tried to pretend, wiping away their stifled tears. They were putting their two middle children on a train to be given to strangers in a desperate attempt to save their lives.

And then there was the trauma of a journey filled with hundreds of children with large luggage labels attached to their coats – human cargo, all in similar circumstances, some excited and noisy at the prospect of their big adventure, some terrified, sobbing, vomiting and those just mute with fear.

Their arrival in the United Kingdom is described by my mother. I have the small check green and black tweed diary with just a few pages written in English, in carefully managed English script. She said:

I remember every detail as if it were yesterday. The train journey to London was very boring. It was a Monday morning of the 3rd of December 1938. I was tired and stiff with cold in the lounge hall in Haringay which was really a summer camp. A slip of paper was given to me with the following words printed on: CARLEBACH girl

To HERMAN Mrs
29, Fountayne Rd.
London, N16,

I stared at the piece of paper, it meant nothing to me yet, and a cot!

The train stopped. Bulli (my mother's nickname for her brother) and I got out, looking around, a bit bewildered. Then we saw two ladies come towards us. One tall rather stout with heaps of make-up on and another, a lot smaller. 'I wonder which is for me,' I whispered to Bulli. Then the lady with the make-up came towards me and kissed me, which struck me as most comical. Why on earth should she kiss somebody she had never in life seen before? A lady from some committee or other came up towards us and started carrying on about something, I couldn't understand. Then the lady, who asked me to call her Aunty, told us to come along. She seemed awfully nice, but she made me feel awfully shy. Perhaps it was the make-up I seemed to notice it more than anything. There was a car waiting for us outside the station. We dropped Bulli off first.

And yes, she was lucky. She was blessed with a kind and loving foster mother who tried to give the little foreign child a home. But the damage was already done. The tearing away of a sensitive child from a place of love and safety must have been deeply injurious to her, like the severing of sheets of delicate tissue paper or the gossamer wings of a butterfly.

While Judith tried to adapt to life in her new home, her brother's situation was not so safe. He had been placed with a religious family who had been considered, on paper, to be

Judith just before she left Germany

suitable. He went to school and tried to live a life of normality. But one day he arrived home to find his possessions outside the door and the house locked and bolted. I don't know the reason. I suspect these people fled the Blitz. But they left my mother's brother at the doorstep with no money, no food, and no way of fending for himself. Even he admitted that for a while he went off the rails just to cope. Obviously this distressed Judith.

And then just as she was feeling a little more secure – she even won the school literature prize in her adoptive language, at the age of almost 16 years – the authorities declared that she was an enemy alien. She had to report to the police station weekly, quit school, and leave her precious foster-mother to find a post to support herself. So that she could eat kosher food she was allocated a job as a scullery maid in a Jewish house.

While she was there she heard that her father and mother and her three littlest sisters had been murdered in Riga. Her father was Rabbi Joseph Zvi Carlebach (1883-1942). He was the last of the orthodox rabbis in Germany and served in Hamburg as Chief Rabbi until his murder in 1942. He and his wife and three youngest girls were forced into a cattle truck and travelled from Hamburg to Riga. When they arrived, they were taken to a nearby ice-covered forest, ordered to dig their own graves, to strip, and were then shot. Then some of the other camp members were ordered to remove all their effects and lime was thrown over the bodies.

Martin Gilbert describes the scene, including factual reports of the time, in his brilliant but terrifyingly honest account of the time in *The Holocaust – the Jewish Tragedy*.

He says that: *As a result of the pressure of those who hoped for better conditions away from Riga, four hundred more Jews than the SS had asked for left the city that Sunday, March 26. They were taken not to a distant labour camp but to the nearby Bikernieker Forest. On the following*

48

day, several trucks entered the Riga Ghetto, and were unloaded. Their cargo was an assortment of personal effects of the people who had been resettled. There were clothes that had been hurriedly taken off by their owners – still turned inside out – stockings attached to girdles and shoes encrusted with mud. The trucks also yielded nursing bottles, children's toys, eye-glasses, bags filled with food and satchels containing photographs and documents.'

The women from the ghetto were ordered to sort out the clothes. The best items were to be sent to Germany, the rest to be distributed among the inmates of the ghetto. Gertrude Schneider, in Journey into Terror, later recalled how, as the women worked at the sorting, 'they recognised many of the clothes, some by the names that had been sewed into them, some by the identity cards still in the pockets, and there were of course, dresses, coats and suits they had seen on their friends and neighbours when they had left the ghetto only a few days before.' Her account continued: 'Soon everyone knew about the cargo that the trucks had brought and about the conditions of the clothes. It did not take any great imagination to understand what had happened to their owners. No longer did anyone scoff at the tales of the Latvian Jews nor think that this could only happen to Ostjuden and never to the Jews from Germany. In many houses, in the ghetto, Kaddish, the Hebrew prayer for the dead, was recited. The German Ghetto was plunged into despair.' Schneider, Journey into Terror, pages 56-58

Among those murdered at the Bikernieker forest that day was Chief Rabbi Joseph Carlebach. Gilbert, The Holocaust – the Jewish Tragedy, p.313.

How could this child cope with her own future?

Her employers in her new home were not sympathetic. As far as they were concerned they were giving a refugee a job and a bed and she should be grateful to them for their kindness. My mother told me that when her own mother came over as the Chief Rabbi's wife on a temporary visit to see her family, (sadly returning to her husband and her death), this very important Jewish lady was shown to her daughter's room in the servants' quarters in the attic. That must have been about 1941. Generally, my mother was treated badly – the details have been lost in the mists of memory. Eventually she could stand no more and falsified her age to join the fire-service. She was only five foot and fine-boned and yet she managed to drive a massive hose-laying lorry. She talked about the driving lessons when they placed a full bowl of water on her lap as she drove, to teach her care in driving. And her courage was rewarded. There were unwritten rules at the station, one of them being that you always brought your wagon home after a shout whatever the circumstances. Once during a bombing attack the fire-engine was damaged. She was aghast when she discovered that the steering wheel had gone, indeed most probably the rest of the engine was not that safe to drive, but she managed to bring it back to the station with the help of a large spanner as replacement for a steering wheel, to tumultuous applause.

Judith during her time with the fire service

By this time her dear elder sister – whom she idolised and had always been her comforter at night if she had a bad dream – had arrived in the United Kingdom on a domestic permit. After a short while this sister volunteered to drive an ambulance (and has been volunteering and helping in the medical profession ever since).

In the meantime, Judith found lodgings in a Jewish boarding house in London. My father had just arrived there and, sitting around the boarding-house table on his first night, discovered over his first war-time-ration-shared supper that there was a Jewish girl upstairs who was suffering from scarlet fever.

'How many days has she been there? How is she?' he asked.

Shoulders shrugged – it was the war. They were afraid of catching the disease.

'You mean to say that there is a Jewish girl upstairs and no one has bothered to take up even a cup of tea?'

In a fit of bravado, my father made his way up to take tea and toast to the invalid. It is said that he fell in love with her instantly. That he returned with flowers and a stick of kosher salami and proposed. My mother said that she rebuked his advances saying: 'You haven't seen my legs yet!' But of course Geoffrey became 'The Rescuer', the Knight in Shining Armour who came at a time of illness with presents and love and the promise of a better life. The idealised romantic dream.

Even so, despite her loneliness, and her need for a special person in her life, she did have misgivings about their prospects. She recovered from her illness and began to doubt their future together. But he persisted. He courted her with flowers and tins of fruit and the occasional bar of chocolate he'd managed to get on the black market. It was always with things that my father showed affection. Years later, she told me that she knew from the start that they had no chance; they came from such different backgrounds. He was the son of simple farming folk who kept a drinking establishment – a type of pub – on the East German/Czech/Polish border. The boundaries changed with each new invader. His mother, my grandmother, was a rough hard woman who told me her stories of the Cossacks and their purges of the Jewish folk, and then the Pogroms when the Polish people needed to find a scapegoat or simply a focus for their unrest and desperate poverty. Jews were always a good target. My father spoke a rougher dialect than Judith's elegant Hoch Deutch. But he wanted her and flattered her ego. She was vulnerable and, one night in the underground, he proposed to her again and she accepted. And when she had misgivings soon after her acceptance, he threatened suicide. She was trapped.

There were no parents under the Chuppah (marriage canopy) to stand by her side. From the photographs it looks as if her elder sister and brother were substitute parents. I have a precious yellowing photograph which shows a young pretty woman: dark haired with a kink in the curls above the forehead, just as I have now. She is wearing an expression of anxiety, uncertainty, not uncommon in a bride, but for a wedding photograph – my father is the thin young handsome man standing next to her – there is a conspicuous absence of joy. There is no glow. She is not a radiant bride. There is wistfulness, a sadness of expression that almost foretells her expectations. She is dressed in a sensible navy suit decorated with a corsage of white carnations, and a small cheap veil hangs from a white ornament in her hair. I know my mother. She must have been sad not to have the money or the coupons to buy a proper wedding dress. Or was she still mourning the loss of her parents and maybe felt that a white dress was inappropriate? My mother was very particular about presenting herself in appropriate clothes. But I'm sure she would have wanted to look the part of a bride. She often went to the pictures with her sister and later her husband. Years later I heard the stories of how Ronald Colman and

Greer Garson stole her imagination in *Blossoms in the Dust*. How Celia Johnson and Trevor Howard championed her thoughts and her soul in *Brief Encounter*. That she would think of those magical people and their lives would transport her to another world. Years later we would watch the old films together in her bedroom and I would see her face change as, for a short time, she became that Hollywood character. I'm sure practicality and lack of finances decided her dress that day.

Sadly not even the reception went as planned. The night before the wedding, the synagogue was bombed and the food that had been assembled from collected coupons from friends and relations was lost. The pair, together with Judith's sister and brother, carried the wedding cake on the tube to another synagogue where my cousin officiated and married them.

My mother continued to relish her work in the fire-service. She enjoyed the fact that she was performing an essential function and enjoyed the safe flirtation and banter of working among men. She had friends and the company of some of her family who had managed to escape Germany before the Holocaust. But my father was terrified of the bombs. He could not cope and cried like a child, so I have been told, covering his hands with his ears and shaking at the sound of a siren. So they moved away from her friends and family to Gateshead – the focus of religious Jewry at that time. There my mother hoped my father would study religious books and begin to enjoy the beauty of the religion. In fact, become more like the man she needed in her life. He began to work with a Rabbi. They became part of the community and there I was conceived and born.

However, soon after my difficult birth in 1946 my parents heard that my father's parents had been released from Theresienstadt concentration camp in Germany. My grandmother had spent her days thinking of her son in England who would care for them when they were released.

There was very little else to dispel the hunger pangs apart from praying for freedom.

The scene has entered the annals of family legend. How my mother watched as a woman of small stature but broad-boned and with a prominent limp arrived, tap-tapping a walking stick over her polished tiles. How my grandmother regarded this young religious woman with disdain. My grandmother would have seen a young orthodox Jewish woman with her hair totally covered with a scarf as decreed by her religious standards, outstretching her arms to her new mother. Of course I don't know my mother's preparations for her visit. But I did know my mother and I am sure that, even with their lack of financial resources, she would have prepared special food. There would have been cut flowers around the house and the whole would look as festive as she could make it.

It must have been a terrible shock for Judith when my grandmother reacted with anger. Because my father was so fearful of his mother, he had never warned her that he had a wife. Not only a wife but a young baby. My grandmother screamed with fury and waved her stick at the young girl.

It is easy to make excuses for the old lady and her husband. She had been in a concentration camp, witnessing barbed-wire horror and starvation. She had spent time in the concentration hospital, which was a dangerous place to be, as many of those who were sick were removed and used for experimental purposes. Each day must have been fraught with terror. She must have witnessed people she had known die before her eyes. She was a spectator to beatings, rape and torture, knowing that at any time it could be her turn. And at last she was released, with her husband, and allowed to journey to a new country where she knew her son was living in comparative safety. He presented her with a wife and a child who were the new focus of his life. Any normal grandmother would have been delighted, but this was not a normal woman, neither were these normal times.

Instead, she screamed with fury at his new family, waving her stick and terrifying my mother. She would not have made any effort to compromise. I know from my own experience that my grandmother was a hard woman. She boasted of beating her children daily. The strap, she believed, was the way to discipline a family of boys.

'That is in case you do something bad today,' my grandmother would say, as my father rose to the pain of the belt.

Despite her incarceration, my grandmother arrived at my parents' small house still full of spirit to fight on. The target for her animosity would now become my mother. First she threatened her with her stick, and then, a few days later when my mother was out, she parted my parents' beds that lay loving-close together. Grandma accused them of living like gypsies. And every day she mocked my mother's religious beliefs, blaming her and her like as the cause of the Holocaust.

To my mother, the Sabbath preparations were more than just making some food, they were a weekly remembrance of everything that had been precious in her life. But now she was watched and laughed at and called 'Die Fromme', the religious one. And my grandmother soon found that telling my mother lurid stories of the camps could easily reduce her to tears. She knew, of course, that my mother's parents, sisters and many uncles, aunts and friends had suffered similar tortures and worse.

Eventually the situation became untenable. My mother was afraid of living with this woman, and one tearful day found a map of the British Isles and stuck a pin in the place she thought was the least accessible to the old lady, with an active Jewish community. In the frozen winter of 1947 my parents moved from Newcastle to Cardiff with an eighteen month baby. The young girl who craved roots and a large loving family was once more drowning in a pool of loneliness. More than anything she yearned to be part of a loving group and to be wanted. But again she was forced into isolation.

They moved into one of the poorer areas of Cardiff. It is strange to me that the place they found to live was so far away from a synagogue. But perhaps that was all they could afford or, maybe, it was sheer lack of knowledge and haste in trying to establish a base that made their purchase so wrong. Probably my father went on ahead and just found an inexpensive property and bought it without consulting my mother. There are no records to explain it. So they lived on the outskirts of Cardiff and gradually they became known to the rest of the community. My mother was an attractive woman and quickly made friends. But there is sometimes a superficiality to new friendships. Closeness and deep friendship requires time, small returned favours, the exchange of experience, empathy. And loneliness encourages poor friendships. So this now plump young girl who hated her postnatal size became friendly with a smart young woman, let us call her Celia, (not her real name but she is still alive), who talked of little but clothes, the latest fashions, the films and getting slimmer. To her applause my mother learnt the conjuring tricks of slimness. The black coffee and lemon juice, the skipped meals – 'No, I couldn't possibly eat breakfast, I find it lies too heavy' – or the 'No, I can't. I had a huge lunch!' She was chasing the temptations of lean equals beautiful, learning new and ugly starvation techniques that would result in, she thought, the approval or envy of her peers. She wanted to be one of them. She needed to be popular and slimness would be more acceptable to that group and, in particular, that woman. She was intelligent and determined, so she did it better. Her methods were more effective, more long-lasting and more successful than anyone else's. At the same time she was extraordinarily innocent. Up until her death, she always believed that anything that anyone told her was true. How could she have discovered otherwise? Her ability to understand people had been damaged. And my father was certainly not in a position to help her understand her friends, as for the most part he resented her position within any group. The more successful and popular she became, the more vulnerable he felt. He always underestimated her loyalty and love.

So many people have since told me how, at that time, her brightness and vivacity shone through. Many have said that it was as if a light suddenly flooded a dark space when she entered a room, and that she was able to transform any average experience into an event.

But in order to be part of her chosen group, she needed to follow the rules they laid down. And if the 'New Look' waist prescribed by Christian Dior in 1947 would suit her and make her more attractive, more interesting, then she would starve herself into that shape – encouraged by her peers.

I used to own one of her dresses. A very special dress that sat in the wardrobe with its attendant clusters of mothballs, polythene bags, and anxieties that in some way it could become damaged. (I have now donated it to the costume department of the Museum of Welsh Life at St. Fagans so that all can enjoy its beauty, especially fashion students.) She bought it in a shop in London where the stars of the day sold their once or twice-worn clothes. It was her way of buying designer clothes without paying the true cost. I remember her when I was very young: she was a blonde, now, and was wearing the shot black taffeta, calf-length ball gown. It skimmed her perfect shoulders and was darted into a perfect twenty-three inch waist. Appliqué'd velvet scrolls curved from the waist, curling down the full skirt, emphasising the minuteness of her waist and at the same time revelling in the excessiveness of cloth needed for the design. It was Dior's way of celebrating the end of fabric restrictions after the Second World War. And of course there was every reason to buy such a garment as there were many balls and dances to attend within the community. My mother loved to dance, so I'm sure she felt justified in its purchase.

However, knowing her, I'm sure she would have been able to copy the pattern once seen, as one of her many talents was dressmaking. She adored fabrics and had perfect taste. With very little money she would create her own style. Black cardigans were worn backwards and good imitation pearls were twisted round her slim neck and hung down the slope of her back. She always wore hats, gloves and bags to match and her make-up would be perfectly applied. She was a kind of blonde Audrey Hepburn with the same elegance, coupled with a constant need for perfection in everything she did, from throwing a party to dressing to go out. She once made herself a strapless evening top by covering an old waist-length strapless bra with the petals from bunches of artificial roses and sewing them petal by petal on to the bra. Then she added rhinestones and pearls and set them into the centres of the petals. The whole process took hours but she had such a talent to create beautiful things. Sadly I have only the photograph. I wish I possessed the garment.

She would also wear shoes of amazing height. Sometimes she bought them from the same shop as the designer dress. I'd hear her say, 'Oh these are so comfortable', and then when no one was looking slip them off her feet and rub sore toes or ankles. She never admitted to pain.

I think she believed that, if she could not achieve perfection in her life, she could make her body perfect.

Very soon after their arrival in Cardiff, my mother set up a small business selling clothes. My father had been working as a pattern cutter for one of his uncles. But he hated his whole situation and resented the blanket of responsibility that, he felt, suffocated his life, dreaming of a life as a farmer or a vet. He often told me how he had begun studying for these exams, and longed for the countryside where his poor communication skills would not be under scrutiny. I once heard him talking to a pathologist and saying how he envied his job. 'At least all your customers are dead ones,' he muttered.

Now, though, he would join my mother. This young woman with the energy of a bee and the same love of work had initiated a career for him, in a small city, and manacled all his dreams of escape by binding him to a life of concrete and small women's 'Madame shops'.

My mother became an elegant fashionista. And the perfect clothes horse. Size ten, then eight, then six became the mandatory size in the wardrobe, and the ideal was set. When I was still quite young she was buying in for their business in London. I'd watch the preparations for her journeys – the perfectly applied makeup, each set pin-curl unclipped and fingered carefully in its place and then a heavy mist of lacquer spray-setting the image. She would kiss me and leave, sporting a perfect hat, and leather gloves to match the bag, small fragrant, beautiful, determined.

And, yes, they progressed. Thanks to her resolve, they moved out of one of the poorest areas of Cardiff to pleasant leafy suburbia and Penylan, and to the still comparatively pleasant moments of my childhood.

But is this fair, so much admiration of my mother, and denigration of my father? My father, tragically, was born of abusive parents whose lives were set in poverty and persecution. His mother was desperately disappointed when she had a second boy. She refused to have his long golden ringlets cut and dressed him in girls' clothes, sending him to his first day of school in them. After hours of ridicule, he left and made his way home via the barber's, instructing him to shave all his hair off. When he returned home he was beaten. My grandmother boasted to me of the strangeness of her son, of how as a child he found a litter of kittens in the village where they lived, and drowned them all so that he could watch the bubbles coming to the top of the bucket. She thought it was amusing. She was primarily a business woman who ran a pub and could not be bothered with her second son. No one explained to the young boy about cruelty, and that is what he received in daily doses.

His older brother was adored. The first son, the precious one, the hope of the family. He was sent at great expense to the University of Perugia. My father didn't get a very good start in education, and most probably because of his difficult behaviour, it was decided that he was safer working with cattle.

But Dad had talents that were never encouraged or developed. He was very musical and could play any instrument and any tune after just hearing the notes. He played the harmonica and the accordion with great feeling, but it was rare to hear him play. Sometimes for the Jewish festival of lights – Chanukah – my mother would persuade him to open the box that held the accordion and I'd watch his broad-wristed small hands caress the ivory keys. He would play with forced jollity but the mood never lasted beyond the first verse and the instrument would be returned in anger, more often than not. His voice would have matched any fifties crooner's voice and if we occasionally heard him singing, my mother and I would nudge each other and whisper that Daddy was in a good mood.

My mother loved to find a new interest. One month it might be pen and ink drawing, the next month pottery. During her pottery phase, she ordered the clay and some basic tools. One very precious afternoon, we all sat together in the kitchen. My mother slabbed an extraordinary pot: a modern shape, functional and elegant. After much protest, my father sat with us. My mother handed him a lump of clay which he kneaded and kneaded and then, as if his hands had always known the medium, he began to work the clay, humming a tune under his breath. Gradually, the soft-eyed head and curved spine of a cow lying down emerged.

'Daddy, Daddy,' I shouted in admiration, 'I didn't know you were so clever!'

I dragged my seat around to his side watching the soft roll of underbelly and elegantly structured legs emerge.

'It's beautiful, Daddy. Please can I keep it? Can I keep it? Have it in my room?'

The clay cow sat on my mother's kitchen top drying. I'd look at it from time to time, marvelling at its perfection. I thought it was one of the most beautiful things I'd ever seen. As it dried from sticky clay into a hardened sculpture, I checked to see when I could move it into my room. Then one day I came home from school and my father was home early. For a few seconds I was pleased to see him. Then I felt his mood, as if the black of a storm darkened a summer-lit room. I knew it was time to stay quiet, curl in my corner and make a show of being involved in homework, occupied, not to antagonise the angry beast churning inside him. But it was to no avail. As usual his shouting reduced my mother to tears and she began to be sick, looking at him with accusing eyes. The angry monster inside him unleashed its full fury and he smashed the cow.

We know the child that shatters the faces of his sister's dolls when she shows them love. The young lad compelled to kick and stamp down daffodils in a park's summer display, mistaking them for privilege instead of a gift for everyone. The older delinquent who has to damage and hurt, whether it is a key scraped across someone's car or property, or the beating or worse of another person. In those few minutes all those people were my father.

This chapter has been particularly difficult to write and it is only the distance of years that that enables me to do so now. For such a long time I buried his rage, not able to be angry myself. Quietly telling myself that silence was the best course. That peace would be mine if I forgot. But peace was never achieved. Memory, triggered by a few bars of music,

61

the sight of a head from the back in a coffee shop – 'good gracious, that looks so like…' – and the odour of vomit, ensures that the past hangs on my shoulders like a heavy jacket. And so I have had to search for the truth. Make a map of my wounds and by exhuming and defining them, make the route less painful. By giving the problems an identity they are no longer hidden away. And that is important. I have to move on. I am their child and possess some of their traits and weaknesses. If I am over-sensitive, for instance, I know that this vulnerability was also part of my mother's makeup. However, I have not inherited my father's rages. In fact I find it difficult to express anger. In the base of my belly is a place where those emotions are created. I watch people who are angry and throw words about, red-faced. Only three times in my adult life have I managed to express such feelings, but I watch my grandchildren and pray that they will be blessed with more balance in their lives. That if they are hurt they will be able to express and understand that hurt, and not destroy for the sake of articulation. By today's standards, both my parents were asylum seekers – running away from certain death. But for them and others like them, escape is not sufficient. There has to be a future. To die years later without satisfaction is to merely exist until that moment of demise. And to have children within that situation risks passing on those desperate needs. Later, even though my parents were dead, I continued suffering on their behalf.

Did our lives improve? As a train without brakes hurtles into a Stygian tunnel.

Chapter Five

Hospital Fish

I was thirteen and had learnt to live a clandestine existence.
Like the dream house. The shell, the epitome of modernity.
Something to catch the eye and symbolise the cultural
elegance that was my mother. But inside, a putrid mix of
despair and sickness, growing daily. We still maintained that
outside-world exterior, however, a kind of skin of normality.
We were the happy happy family and Mummy was a bit
poorly. People asked questions:

'And how is Judith…your poor mother?'

'Oh, she's about the same.'

The words kept the secret and no one knew.

Our routine was ruled by my mother's pains and, when
my father was absent, they would approach a ghastly climax
in the early hours of the morning. Geoffrey was now a
manufacturer's agent and would spend weeks away at a
time, coming home just at weekends to change his clothes
collections, which he showed to buyers in small shops all
over Wales and the West Country, and pick up fresh shirts
for himself. Sometimes during the week I would be able to
go to bed and sleep for a few hours but, inevitably, she
would call. In the beginning, she would suddenly appear at
my door gasping.

'Darling, darling I'm so ill. You've got to…'

I'd wake with a start. She'd be fainting and trying to
hold on to my door.

'Darling. I feel so bad.'

Sometimes I'd have to catch her before she fell. I'd
carry her to her bed and lift her on to the pink candy-striped

sheets she loved. And she'd be gasping and twisting her thin body as the pain contorted her tired muscles. Unfortunately malnutrition caused by starvation means a lack of potassium, calcium and magnesium, which are necessary to keep the body functioning. Without those vital elements terrible cramps, at the very least, occur.

She would faint in and out of consciousness. I would be so fearful. I would go downstairs for hot water mixed with Valerian drops that smelt of rat poison and seemed to be as difficult to swallow, to pacify the palpitations.

'Mummy, you're so bad. Shall I call the doctor?'

'No! Not the doctor,' she'd gasp. 'He'll send me to hospital!'

We'd battle through those desperate dark hours. I emptied bed-pans and vomit bowls with my own body retching at the smell, and then boiled the kettle again and again for hot drinks, hot water bottles,

'I'm so cold.' The shivers would shake her body.

Ice out of the fridge – 'Darling, I'm so hot!' – as she threw off sheets, her body burning, and I'd pray that my father would come home early, and that she would be better. And, in the bad bad hours, that she would just let me ring the doctor.

Oddly, I was always aware of the seasons outside. The excited chatter of birds in the spring. Birds were one of my links with the outside world – my feathery metaphor for freedom. Sometimes on the way to school or watching the pink streaks of a dawn across a violet sky, after a bad night, I'd hear the easy chatter of blue tits nesting. It became an obsession to watch the birds and I still enjoy that passion. They had plans and lived every day with hope.

On my way to school, sometimes with little or even no sleep, I'd pray to my G-d, to help me – pleading to make our lives a little easier. I would be so needy for sleep, tired all the time, with constant complaints from my teachers.

'Could do better. Could have learnt the poem better. Why was this piece not completed?'

Only when she saw she was losing her grip on reality, or she could not walk at all, would I be allowed to call the doctor (in those days our G.P. would still come out in the middle of the night). I'd phone to a chorus of tears, and shuddering cries, and after a very few minutes our faithful doctor would appear on our doorstep. I'd watch his sleep-tired face grow green when he saw the sight of my poor mother and, after a cursory examination, a check of pupils, pulse and blood pressure, the call for the ambulance always followed. I've lost count of the times my mother was taken into hospital. I've lost count of the times I swayed in an ambulance fearful that this time we had left it too late. Or been asked, on admission – a young school-girl – to remember all the drugs taken daily by my mother. Each time I felt guilty that I was relieved to see her in the green-grey painted surroundings with the oh so jolly curtains surrounding her bed, even though I knew she hated the place. I was simply grateful for a few nights' sleep and that someone cleverer than me would be in charge of her wellbeing. But I never managed to dump the guilt of delivering her to the place she hated so much.

This stupid guilt that I understand now, but did not then, was exacerbated by my father's anger when he would finally arrive. I was afraid to ring him myself, and always hoped that a kindly matron or staff sister would do it. But he would be difficult to reach as he never gave us an itinerary and I could only guess from past conversations at the places he might be staying. It was a matter of ringing around hotels asking if my father was staying there. Eventually he would be found and then I would dread hearing his footsteps walking heavy on polished lino'd floors. His shouting through hushed corridors and demanding to see his wife. I could always hear him well before he arrived and I would be afraid. Sometimes, not always – it depended on his mood –

he would look accusingly across the bed to me. I had spoilt his trip. He'd had to cancel appointments. It would mean that he'd have to go back to clients, we would lose money. His eyes said it all.

But then his mood would change and he would gaze at my mother, now stabilized, with a drip pumping some kind of solution, usually plasma, into the hollow cave of her body. She'd look at him, needing love, and show him the bracelets of bruises around her wrists. Sometimes he would be tender and make an attempt to kiss her. Or make a show of handing her the largest bouquet of flowers ever seen. Too heavy for her to lift and she would be made happy by this display of love – her Geoffrey would be back. He would dispense bunches from the bouquet around the ward for those who had none.

Sometimes he'd throw a jewellery box on to the hospital bed. I'd watch her, coy, like a new lover or bride, pick up the parcel and coo with appreciation. The conversation was always the same.

'Oh Geoffrey, how wonderful. You shouldn't throw a beautiful thing like that on the bed. How did you find time with all your work? Oh look, Ruthie…better take it home…it's not fair to have this in front of poor people who have nothing.'

How I hated those guilt presents – the small seed-pearl brooch set in the shape of a swallow caught in flight, and the fine diamond necklace with its centre of a red enamelled heart. She loved that piece and wore it often. To me it signified her broken heart.

At last, with the help of intravenous liquids, enforced pieces of toast, and copious cups of milky tea, my mother would be stabilized and sent home. Within days my father would be muttering about the loss of business and how he had to make up appointments. And we would climb back on to the merry-go-round of absences and sickness.

Any peace-offering gift would make its way home and into my mother's cream leather jewellery box, with every likelihood that it would be worn only in the house. She might use it when she dressed for her trip downstairs to sit in her big chair, when on occasions her oldest and most faithful friend would call. She would try to balance those bird-bones on the hardness of the stool in front of the dressing table, only for seconds, as it was painful just to sit. She would select her jewellery as if she were back in the old times and she was entertaining a mass of friends. The rings would be worn on fingers whose nails were perfectly manicured and polished. And a fine necklace would hang about her tiny neck. Often she would be dressed in a nightdress with the thinnest wool wrap over her body. Anything heavy would be impossible to wear and could cause pressure sores. And because she lived in the thinnest of clothes, the house was always heated to hospital-hot temperatures.

When she was still able to move a little, she would spend hours in the preparation of tea for friends – her special event. She would sit on a stool in her blue and white kitchen and tell me what she wanted to make. While she watched and directed, I would make the tiniest brown bread egg sandwiches with all the crusts cut off. Open rye bread pieces decorated with morsels of smoked salmon or fingers of cucumber with white fine bread. Then maybe a few home-made biscuits or a few fresh scones. With the tray laid with the best cloth and tea-set she would fall into her chair exhausted. But at least for a few hours she was happy, seeing people – just like old times.

I remember one of those days. It must have been a Jewish festival because my mother had asked husbands as well. We'd planned the preparations for weeks. It gave my mother purpose and although she was sick I saw her happy for a few hours. On the day of the tea-party my mother was not so good, so the party was moved into her bedroom. It was a cramped space to seat maybe four men in dark suits and four ladies, but no one seemed to mind and the tea was in full swing. I was running up and down the stairs refilling the tea-pot and thinking it was wonderful to hear people in the house.

Despite the fact that it was a Jewish festival my father was still working and arrived home in the midst of the sounds of laughter and bonhomie. He stormed into the house and heard the chorus of voices emanating from my mother's room. His face grew red. Like a man possessed, he raced up the stairs and burst into the bedroom. My mother was delighted to see him.

'Oh Geoffrey. You've come home in time. How lovely.'

But he was too wrapped up in his jealousy; he ignored her welcome. He screamed at the throng sat around the bed with delicate tea-cups poised on awkward knees, and laughter slowly transforming into shock on their faces.

'Haven't you got anywhere to go?' he screamed. 'Do you think this is a bloody restaurant? Haven't you got food in your own houses?'

They scattered as if his voice had been peppered with gun-shot, picking up coats and hats and racing to get downstairs and out through the door, while my mother lay sobbing in her bed. Days of tears, arguments and recriminations followed that outburst. For a second, as the guests were running away, I tried to stop them, before I saw my father's face and scurried to my bedroom, clasping my hands over my ears, praying that it would soon cease. But I knew that when it stopped, the wisp of the shell that was my mother would be a little sicker. She would be a little thinner and my father would disappear again.

I have tried to forgive him for that hurt.

I was about fourteen when my mother began again to look for cures away from home. She went to a few places in Switzerland and once to Israel to some sanatorium. In her absence I was lonely. I think my mother's friends, apart from a very few, were only too delighted to be free of worrying about 'poor, sick Judith' and so made few enquiries as to my situation. My father would have taken exception to their scrutiny anyway, and condemned them as nosy. When these times coincided with the school holidays, I used to make myself a few sandwiches and walk for hours. I was lucky, for, half a mile away from our house, stretched lanes that led to open countryside. I used to take my paints and enjoy my thoughts sitting on hilly tussocks, watching other worlds – sheep, tractors weaving through corrugated corduroy fields, and hay-making and the orange and green lichens on stones. I'd come home when it was dark. One day I left the house. No one knew where I was. I must have been about twelve as I remember we had not been in our new house for very long. Those magical lanes with their catkins and pussy willows, and then the dog-roses and honeysuckle and bumble-bee-buzzed foxglove, were a huge attraction. But on that day, my wanderings stopped. I was sitting on a mound of rocks near the cry of sheep, enjoying the view, when a stranger began to talk to me. He spoke to me in a gruff voice. He was dressed as a woman but was undoubtedly a man. I had never seen anyone like that before. no one had ever explained anything like that to me. I felt afraid. I'm sure now that he was totally innocent. But as my only references were Enid Blyton, the mysteries of *Black Beauty, David Copperfield* and *Grimms' Fairy Tales,* I had no adult knowledge to judge by. I can remember running away, terrified at his broad hair-covered hands extending through a woman's sleeve. When I returned to the house my father was watching the news. A murder had occurred in the lanes behind our house. In my innocence I blurted out the story of my encounter. Both my father and I connected the two events. I never visited the lanes on my own again, and it was a sad loss to me.

I realise now how child-like we were, growing up in the early sixties. Most of the girls in my school were as naive as I was. We knew nothing of homosexuality or lesbianism or any sexual deviation. We had no knowledge or experience of sex and most of us were virgins. A very few would boast that 'they had done it' but inside we knew that they were not very nice and that we were not following their example. For to sleep with a boy was to become pregnant and socially damned. There were no sexual references, nothing to assist the unveiling of knowledge, either on the television or the radio, and the programmes that did exist were vetted and excluded by watchful guardians. So our only understanding was gained by staring and giggling at male physiology in books in the library, fostered by febrile discussions at break and embroidered by healthy imaginations. A male friend made a fortune by hiring out a copy of D.H.Lawrence's *Lady Chatterley's Lover* at five shillings 'a go' to all his school friends.

I did not ask my mother about sexual matters. We talked about periods and their painfulness and that was it. But, thinking about it now, I'm not sure that my mother was much more knowledgeable than I was. Certainly, on sexual deviation, she had no idea. If she was well, we listened to the afternoon play on the radio or took a gentle walk around the garden, but there was never any discussion related to my changing body or its needs.

The beats of my life ran according to the rhythms and orders of our crazy house. As each birthday approached in May I'd pray that my mother would get better. For although my mother was desperately ill throughout most of my life, I was always sure that one day her health would improve – that there was a miracle to be had somewhere. One day there would be a new drug. One day we would make the journey to Harley Street and there would be a doctor who would understand my mother's condition and cure her. One day…

One day she was bad. I was about fourteen years old. We had hit the gasping terrors again and there was no space in an NHS hospital. My father was home that time and after swift muttered discussions with our GP, my mother was hurriedly dispatched to a private nursing home. It was run by nuns who flitted about on highly polished corridors like tireless white birds, swooping and creaking over patients. As we trooped in on the first night with flowers and her favourite biscuits, she was propped on pillows. Her eyes were swollen, red with crying. And her arms were blue with bruises where the drip needle attachment had been inserted so many times to find a suitable vein.

'Please Geoff, take me out of this place...I'm so unhappy...You've got to get me out of here...please, love...please.'

But I was grateful that she was being looked after even if just for a few days, and my father was less patient than I, ignoring her protests. Even to this day, I feel badly that I didn't listen more. That my reflexes – my personal warning lights – remained inactive. But she always cried when she went in initially. She felt trapped like a tiny bird locked in a hostile cage. She had none of her comforts: the sheets were rough and her skin was so sensitive that in a matter of hours she would be covered in pressure-sores. Very few realised that she needed frequent fluids and that the jug of bright pseudo orange squash customarily dumped on the locker at the side of her bed would only inflame her acid-sensitised throat.

I tried to bring in foods to tempt her, but there would be those who resented her little parcels, wrapped and labelled in the hospital fridge. Sometimes the food was stolen and inquiries merely resulted in a disparaging sniff and a shrug of shoulders. Staff, who had been given their orders from doctors, insisted that she should eat the hospital food, and would stand over her, watching and noting her input and

71

output until she felt terrorised. There was always one member of staff who was intolerant of her condition.

And then she was Jewish. She kept very strict *Kashrut* and that in itself was a nuisance. She was perceived as being difficult. She was stereotyped as the awkward Jew who was spoilt. A trouble-maker who wouldn't even eat the fish. I heard the conversations, choked on the sour hostility, tasting the pain of that bitter-fruit myself.

'What do you mean you can't – you said you can't eat the meat? Well, you can eat chicken…well then, the fish, that's got to be alright. All your race eat the fish. How do we know if it has fins and scales? It comes in from the kitchen – it's hospital fish.'

Later, we tried to laugh at the thought of a special 'hospital fish' that swam in a white coat with a stethoscope curling around its scaly exterior, but, that day, the scene finished in a blaring silence that deafened my terrified mother and a gleam of triumph off stage as the Jewess was duly admonished, stuck with labels and dumped in the pigeon-hole marked 'awkward'. I have experienced such difficulties in hospital myself. But it is more serious when you are five stone of bones and vulnerability. When you ask for more pillows to lie on and they brand you the Princess from the fairytale who can't cope with the pea, and then bring you pillows so hard and inflexible they make your head ache.

There was a lower level of tolerance and understanding about ethnic minorities in those days, and if there were undercurrents of ill feeling, they would be exposed.

The afternoon after she was admitted we returned. The scent of sickly sweet flowers was overwhelming as we passed the little chapel with the figure of the crucified Christ bleeding and hanging, nailed on the cross. We walked down endless polished corridors, my father always ahead striding as if he had lived there all his life, me trying to keep up, uncomfortable at the dead-staring visions of crucifix and stiff carved marble saints. The smell of institutional cleaning fluids always made me gag. Finally we turned into the 'four-bedder' where my mother lay. I had never seen my mother quite so distraught before. I wanted to hug her, to pacify her, to tell her that the nuns were only trying to make her better. She was hysterical, begging my father to take her away. He did nothing. I did nothing.

I regret, I regret.

A couple of days later, my mother managed to persuade one of the orderlies to push her in a wheelchair to the phone. I had just come home from school. I picked up the receiver, overjoyed to hear her voice.

'Mummy, Mummy, you must be feeling better. I'm so thrilled. Are they making you better?' A stupid, facile question.

She answered in a different voice – a growling cry from the depths of her soul, tears flooding.

'Tell Daddy, please, when he rings. He's got to come and get me. There's an old woman in the next bed – she's got knives – I'm terrified – I can't sleep – I can't eat – I…'

'But how has she got the knives?'

'She's stolen them from the kitchen!'

I regret, I regret. I should have nagged, cajoled, persuaded.

My father walked in from work in a relatively pleasant mood. I told him.

'It's the drugs – she's dreaming – she'll get over it.'

I did try to insist but I was young, only fourteen, and my words were blown away.

So I prepared my tiny sandwiches to take in later, with the crusts cut off to spoil her and a flask of fat-free home-made chicken soup and vegetables cut into inch dice to tempt.

She was sobbing and waved one accusing finger.

'I told you to tell Daddy about the woman. I told you.'

Next to my mother was an empty bed. Between sobs she told us that they had placed a very old woman with senile dementia in there. They had been warned that she was dangerous. In the curtained dark, as the night staff checked the far wards, the old lady had crawled out of her bed and discovered the kitchen. She removed numerous carving knives which they later found secreted in her bedclothes. Fortunately nothing happened to my mother but we had left her for nights in a state of rigid anguish, with that woman next to her. As we left that evening, we saw the old lady in a single side ward, the sides of the bed elevated like a cage, her withered arms tied to the sides with bandages, twitching and pulling in desperation.

The next day, my father left to go away. He told me that I could take a taxi to visit my mother. She was stable now. I never considered my own situation – being alone in the house. There was a house-keeper who attended to some jobs in the house but she was not interested in me and would leave to look after her own family. I tried to understand my father's behaviour. I know he was afraid of the situation. It was safer to be an ostrich or to run away. Was he back with the shells that fell about his ears in the war? Was he running away again from a danger far greater than his mother's bullying? Whichever, he now had the perfect excuse. His fashion work took him to Devon, Cornwall, West Wales, Mid-Wales and the Valleys, where the owners of small 'Madame shops' would welcome his charms. He could talk to these women and call them 'Darling' even if under his breath they were all 'cows'. At least that's what he told my mother.

So, in my father's absence, a taxi dropped me outside the nursing home in Llandaff. I made my way along the mixed scents of damp sluice, Jeyes Fluid and old flower water, moving quickly past the room where the screens were always pulled tight but the moans seemed louder on each visit, to find my mother propped on pillows, her face looking sore. Her eyes were reddened and swollen yet again. My insides heaved with despair. I knew that there would be another crisis. Between hiccupping tears she told me how one sister with the help of others had tried to remove the eye-makeup from under her eyes. She never wore any.

'They came with creams and said that I had to take off the make-up from my eyes – I tried to tell them that they had always been like that since I had been poorly but no one would listen. And when I wouldn't take off the black myself, they said that they would do it for me. They pulled me down and rubbed really hard…'

Since my mother's sickness had begun, apart from the painful hollows carved in her thin face and the too-tight skin that gave it, it seemed, too many teeth, she had had panda eyes. That is the only way I can describe them. It was as if she had painted the hollows underneath her eyes with black Kohl. But of course she hadn't. Even at that age, I was horrified at such intolerance and cruelty. I have never spoken about this hurt before but it has simmered below my skin, pulsing now and again like a boil ready to burst.

As has another, verbal this time, uttered to me with sweet sincerity and never articulated until this moment. It was late one afternoon, after school when the lessons had been particularly tough – most probably double maths or physics. I made my way to the ward humming a Guy Mitchell tune to pretend that I was brave. I could do it. Cope with the smell, the marble saints – the fear of finding my mother in some new condition.

I walked quickly past the chapel. The sick-sweet smell of stargazer lilies and chrysanthemums was overwhelming. One of the nuns, who had seemed to like my mother, stopped me.

'Oh my dear,' she said in a soft Irish lilt, her starched habit rustling as she bent forward to speak. Her black eyes like jet glittered out of a well-fed, ruddy complexion.

'My dear, I've talked with the other nuns…we've been praying to our good Lord to take your dear mother.'

I regret, I regret.

My father was absent. I felt so alone. The soft-spoken words banged about the polished corridors like rubber grenades. They bounced back on me, hit the marble saints, crashed on disinfected walls then ricocheted back to me, beating me about my body like missiles.

Somehow, I managed to remove myself from that woman. Walk past her and on to my mother. Somehow I managed to tidy away the horror in my face and present some sort of daughterly smile, along with a few picked flowers from the garden and a replacement flask of soup.

Every day after that I managed to cover my face with a new mask. I had become a grown-up that hid reality from the little girl in the ward in bed. We had exchanged roles. It was up to me to protect her if I could.

Some days I would arrive at her side and she would be sleeping:

'She's had a bad night – she didn't sleep – we've given her something.'

I'd sit by her bed and watch her – her hours were topsy-turvied by white pills and sticky potions. And when she woke, often late in the evening or just when we were leaving at the very end of visiting hours, she'd pray to come home again. But while she was drugged, she was silent – no trouble. I wanted to ask why. Was it so important to sleep every night? Wouldn't it be better to have a reading light and while the hours away so that the next night she would be more tired and fall asleep as expected and a natural sleep pattern would emerge? But I was only a school-girl, a child, hair in brown plaits, dressed in a bottle-green skirt grown shiny from use, smelling of chalk and sour bodies. What use was I? Who would listen to me?

So I'd sit at the side of the bed watching her features twitch as she dreamt and I'd pray that when the drugs lifted she would be well again and her eyes would speak a different story, of terrors past and gone.

But nothing changed. Wherever she went, the tapestry of problems flourished. The warp and weft of anxieties, and trauma, my mother's and ours, combined with the hospital staff's reluctance to accept that my mother was really ill. The consultants and their registrars fell in two categories: those who considered my mother to be shamming – a woman who was bored and needed something to occupy herself, and if she could only pull herself together she could sort out the whole thing herself; and those, in the main the younger ones, who had not yet had the enthusiasm for health care hammered out of their systems, who saw my mother as an 'interesting case' – an experimental rat to cage in their laboratory and play games on with drugs and surgery.

Days ran into weeks. No father around, and no knowing where he was. Isolation. Taxis and different drivers, new faces carrying me in the back of their cars like little Red Riding Hood with my loaded basket of freshly washed nightdress and bed-jacket, thermos flask and home-made treats – scared of the wolf of the day. Walking into wards with my face set in a rehearsed smile. A rictus of hypocrisy. Unwanted intimacies with strangers when secret parts of their bodies were suddenly exposed. A ghastly spin-around where the sight of dying and very sick people became the norm and a discussion of their lives became more important than your own. Where you sat for hours looking out of the window, staring at the outside world, wondering about the buses that passed taking strangers to their homes, to houses with red and blue front doors, loaves of sliced white out in the kitchens, and toast at the sides of fry-ups with brown sauce. I imagined families, dogs and cats, and sometimes laughter.

The background to those day-dreams was the music of sweet female prayers, curling from the chapel around the stone building along the echoing corridors and regular as time. Voices invoking G-d's help in the work to cure the sick and save the world from evil thoughts and heathen invasion. 'Not my G-d,' as I was told by one of the supplicants. 'Another,' they said, paring away my skin from the flesh so they found the essence of heathen. I walked in there so often, past the figures of the saints. But no! My G-d, the same G-d. Just wearing a different hat. Were we so different? And when they spoke, their bright brittle words honed with a steely hardness, did they ever think about a daughter who just loved her Mummy and wanted her home?

My father would return on Friday afternoons. He'd march noisily, high polished shoes on glass polished floors, into the hospital, with bought fancies, flowers and presents and flirt with the nuns – telling them how glamorous and beautiful they looked, much to my embarrassment. He'd stride into the ward, his voice booming before him. My mother's thin face would be flooded with joy – her knight in shining armour had returned. But after a couple of hours he would feign exhaustion. She would tell him to go home and eat. She'd watch his figure disappearing from view, her eyes brimming, trying to follow us as he slammed car doors, and accelerating the car noisily out of the car-park and home. Up the drive to the house and inside. Back in prison. We'd both change into old clothes. Then he'd turn on the television, lay his feet on the padded stool and wait for his food to be served on a trolley in front of him. His eyes would fix on the screen, only breaking away for requests for fruit and dessert and then coffee and cake at ten. I would sit with him as he watched his favourite *Sergeant Bilko* or the antics of *Laurel and Hardy* or the *Keystone Cops*. He would laugh loudly and bash my leg heartily and I would pretend that we were having fun. The same pattern would follow the next day.

Sometimes he'd take me out for lunch to brighten up our weekend. He taught me to eat fish correctly, slipping his knife down the spine like a surgeon and removing the curling back-bone that looked like a cartoon skeleton. He'd lay it on a side-plate with due ceremony.

'People will always know what class you are by the way you eat,' he'd say, deftly slipping exact-sized morsels of buttery fish into his mouth. But he'd always order too much food for me – a massive adult portion – and would be furious if I didn't finish the whole amount. The anger was so intense; he'd shout in the middle of a busy restaurant.

Many times he ordered steak tartare, which he ate regularly at home. I could never understand the attraction of minced raw meat arranged in a large elaborate mound with a raw egg yolk delicately balanced on top, sitting in its shell, garnished with raw onion, anchovies, and capers. I was convinced that the anchovies and capers were there to take the taste away. Once he ordered it for me. I stared at it for ages and the portion seemed to grow larger. My heart started banging with terror at the prospect of yet another public scene and I tried to eat it. Ever the compliant daughter. But it made me gag and my father was furious. He'd ordered it specially and, when I began to refuse, the red colouring my cheeks and the tears beginning to flow, he screamed, 'Now look at the waste!'

It was as if I was rejecting him or a portion of his love by rejecting his food.

We never went out without a row.

Perhaps it was for that reason that I even ate cooked meat when we went out. Even though my mother was very religious and we kept a strictly kosher home, which I ran in my mother's absence, my father managed to persuade me that it was alright to eat meat at a restaurant. I was not stupid. To this day I cannot understand how, as a religious Jew, I was able to live with this destruction of my personal values. It was as if I shut this abuse in a box and put it at the back of my mind. To be silent made for a quieter life.

He lived his life by rules he invented and everyone followed them for harmony. Washing up was executed in a specific order and there would be a row if the rules were broken – glasses first in fresh water, then the dishes rinsed in a separate bowl and then washed after the glasses, then the cutlery and then the pots and pans. Cleaning shoes was done on the kitchen table on top of a layer of the paper from the night before, and the entire shoe was cleaned, especially the small shiny part under the sole – he thought that showed good breeding. His cup of instant coffee was warmed with hot water first and only then could boiling water from the kettle be added. He never drank out of a mug but used a large bone-china cup and saucer. I broke that once. Nothing was thrown away, not used foil or polythene bags – I think our house was the only one in the street where a line of bags and foil hung outside like an alien's washing-line. Even the numbers of lights on in the house at the same time were checked.

In my mother's absence, I dropped painfully into the trench she had dug for me. The status quo was maintained. It was what I thought I should do. My mother was my only example. To the outside world we were still a family of a father, mother and child. Sadly, the mother was not well but was still holding the reins of the home and directing a kind of semaphore to the outside world, who viewed her sickness with a healthy dose of fear and, on the whole, made polite enquiries at a safe distance like via the telephone. I re-dug the trenches. My mother's Thursdays became my Thursdays. The orders for food deliveries were given over the phone. The panic when the meat arrived – would he be happy? And the careful koshering, laying lumps of meat to salt on the wooden slats. I did it all in between maths tests ('could have done better'), English tests, ('has not properly studied the text') and French ('has made no effort this time'). And then there were the hefty Friday preparations of chicken, and chicken soup, chopped liver, and cake. The seamless maintenance of my father's life-style was my goal. To emulate my mother's perfection was my new objective.

Stupid girl. All the time I was searching for praise. Just once I needed him to say 'That was nice,' or 'That was good', or 'I enjoyed that.'

But it never happened. He'd find some fault either in the preparation or in the size of a portion, or something else that probably depended on his week and how he had fared. But I never gave up trying. And I carried on trying, always waiting, hoping for that fleeting word that would show I'd done a good job.

His favourite food was chocolate and vanilla marble cake. I'd have to make it to my mother's standards and as he'd cut into the bitter chocolate swirls enriched with melted chocolate and cocoa, to the sweet vanilla, I'd hold my breath and pray that it would be good enough. Sometimes I'd try to invent something different and with Margerite Pattern's *Baking in Colour*, I'd try coffee and walnut or something else. It had to be just good enough to satisfy the Friday needs but never better, because my mother guarded her place as cake supremo in our family and she would be upset if there was praise. A kind of sticky paranoia ensued if she was away for too long. As if she felt that I might usurp her place in my father's affections.

And as the illness took a hold of my mother, a bizarre trait began to affect her personality. The more sick she became, the more pronounced its manifestation. I could understand that, because of her past, she had an extraordinary need to hold on to possessions. Her books were precious, her clothes, and jewellery. These items gave her a feeling of security, an anchor in a sea of constantly displacing relationships. Her possessions were a raison d'etre, an expression of her personality. Initially, the characteristic was like any other woman who enjoyed her things a little too possessively. But as the illness engulfed her life aspects of her need changed. As a child I was not allowed to wear pink, which was my favourite colour. She was the one who was to wear pink in the house. I was to wear blue or red – both colours which I loathe. But in the fifties your mother dressed you, and made the choices. Very few children growing up at that time had any say in their wardrobe. A fifties child stayed mute and was grateful to be given.

As we both became older, the quirkiness of her need became even more apparent. She was the one that would be good at painting. I was always passionate about my art work but, sadly, she took no pleasure in my teacher's praises and would not entertain the idea that I should study art. That would be her world, her field. If I was found at home picking up a paint-brush I was quickly told that there must be something more useful I could do with my time. Even after I was married, I used to feel a clandestine shiver when faced with a watercolour pad and a sketch book. Perhaps that is why I never felt comfortable with oils, her paints, always preferring the lighter medium of watercolour. When I was nine, one of my mother's friends asked me if I would like a present for my birthday. She'd take me to town and we'd choose it together. It was so exciting. I was never allowed to ask or decide. You had what you were given and in my father's eyes that usually meant encyclopaedias or books on natural history. I said that I would love a paint-box. She took me into town and bought me a watercolour box which I still treasure and use today. But the level of my mother's anger was frightening. I had a terrible row for even asking for a paint-box and, certainly, for saying what I wanted. But it was worth the recriminations. The rich memory of that linseed-scented, dark shop with its mahogany shelves crammed with boxes, brushes and canvasses and the glorious feeling of choosing my own box, still glows in my mind like a Rembrandt canvas.

I did have some toys, dolls, teddies, fuzzy-felts, regular comics, a few board games and a real china tea-set that I was only allowed to play with under supervision. But frequently, when I returned home from school, some of my toys would be gone. When I asked about their disappearance I was told that they were sent to my cousins abroad who had nothing. I never begrudged giving away my things. It was just that I didn't even own my own toys. They were loaned to me, to be disposed of at my mother's discretion.

Later, this idiosyncrasy developed more momentum. It was *her* telephone, *her* sewing things, *her* special biscuits – the thinnest wafers that I was not allowed to touch – and finally *her* doctor. I discovered this last on an occasion when I was physically and mentally exhausted. The backs of my legs ached from running up and down stairs and my back throbbed from carrying my mother to and from the toilet. After a particularly bad week I was in so much pain, I told my mother. She protested. I didn't need to see the doctor. She was the one who saw the doctor. Eventually, after saying that I could not walk except with severe pain, he was called. He diagnosed that both my Achilles tendons were strained and that I had to rest. But there was no one else to care for my mother. My father bought me crepe bandages. I bound my legs and continued running. It was her need to be even more ill than me, on the day the doctor called, which stays in my mind. I had invaded her territory, her persona.

No matter what happened in the house, my father would still leave. It was always the same. Reloading of the stock into the car happened either Saturday night or very early Sunday morning. It was a process that was well known in the fashion industry. Heavy stocks of sample garments would arrive at the showroom in large brown cardboard boxes and would be taken about the country by the likes of my father. They'd travel on specially fitted gown rails in the back of the car, and would be unloaded again on to transportable rails, to be shown in rented hotel rooms in various towns. Each range – and he did coats, rainwear, dresses, suits, knitwear and cocktail-wear – would be taken out of the car, shown for that week or sometimes just one or two days, then returned to the

83

car after showing. On the way to his destination, my father would pick up his model of the week, sometimes a blonde, sometimes a brunette, but always beautiful, with a perfect size twelve body, able to show off the clothes. They would travel together in the garment transport. Hours later, after he had left and I had tried to pacify my mother's tears, he would phone from strange phone boxes where the reception was crackling and filled with bursts of other people's music.

But as I moved into my teens, till fourteen, life was not all bad. Sometimes my mother would seem to be well. She would be blessed with sudden bursts of energy. I would return from school and she was dressed and phoning people. Or we'd have weeks when she was painting: vast canvasses filled with inspired visions of colour and light. She would have been working all day in front of her latest canvas: she painted detailed, vibrant, pictures of landscapes, and townscapes dotted with people and tiny animals, luminous with colour. I would hesitate for seconds at the back door, always worried in case yesterday was just a dream, but then find her standing in the lounge on dust sheets carefully placed over the Persian carpets, very tiny in black leggings with an oversized wildly-coloured shirt hung about her slimness and legs that were no more than a silhouette of bones. The large polished radiogram would be blaring out Beethoven, Rachmaninov, Mendelssohn or Grieg. She would be possessed, detached from me as if I was not there, and sometimes she would sing and her voice was loud and needy. Sometimes I'd find her in the kitchen cooking blissful treats. We would hug.

'Darling, I feel better,' she'd say, patting the flatness between her girdle of bones. She'd pull up the Venetian blinds and light would flood the room and I would hear laughter – sometimes ours – and I'd think that all the nightmares were behind us. That we would start again from that day.

During one burst of new-found energy Mum decided that she needed help to understand the process of self-abuse and maybe cure herself. She instigated a process of analysis with a psychiatrist. They spent hours in her bedroom with the door tightly shut. Then I questioned nothing. Now I feel it's a little odd. The obvious explanation was that there was nowhere else in the open-plan design house to go for privacy. I knocked on the door, delivered trays of tea and coffee and whatever snacks or meals my mother and I had previously prepared, and carefully shut the door behind me. But my father's reaction to this man's invasion within our lives was different. And maybe, on reflection, he had some justification. He hated him. I suspect that within his mind this man was just another of those who had tried to steal her away before. That he felt this man was usurping his place. And even if my father no longer lived in that bedroom or slept with my mother, he believed this man had no place there. Each session made him angrier, so that, eventually, there was a cacophony of slammed doors and tirades of abuse before the doctor arrived. While he was there I'd hear my father shouting up the stairs: 'What are you doing with the bloody bastard? What the hell are you doing up there?' followed by child-like angry sulks after the man had left. It didn't help that the psychiatrist saw my mother after his own daytime practice so that the consultations lasted long into the night.

The days after a session would see my mother flushed with excitement. She'd tell me over coffee why certain aspects of her illness were happening, about her childhood, about her parents' death and my grandmother's place in her anxieties. She wanted to relate the whole discussion to my father but he was not interested. It was obvious that she was also enjoying and grateful for the interest and attention of this man by her bedside.

The weeks passed. I witnessed a marked improvement in my mother's health. Maybe, just maybe, this man held the key that could unlock the box and set my mother free from sickness?

But finally it all became too much for my father. Verbal abuse was not sufficient. He could no longer control his jealousy, and the fact that my mother was improving demonstrated to him that his resentful fears were rooted in some ugly, growing truth.

Four months later when I came home from school, my mother was downstairs sitting in the oversized chair which was covered with sheets and softened with vast pillows to ease the pain. She was hitting her stomach violently and vomiting in between cries of anguish.

'But, Geoff, there was no need. He wasn't – we weren't…'

'That's what you say…I don't trust the bastard, whatever he's up to… and you are paying him good money on top.'

'But, Geoff, I was feeling better…'

'Yes, yes I'm bloody sure you felt better…'

'I was beginning to understand why. The whole thing was making sense.'

Her head and eyes lowered as she tried to catch her breath and vomit at the same time.

'You just don't understand, do you?'

'All I bloody know is that he was in my house in my bedroom with my wife…'

'But he's a doctor…'

Later my mother told me that in the early hours of the morning, when I had fallen into an exhausted sleep recovering from a series of difficult nights, my father had run up the stairs, burst into their patient/doctor session, manhandling the doctor and pulling him by his coat lapels. Mum said that their faces were so near together that she was afraid they would come to blows. It was close. The man never returned.

Chapter Six

Still Fighting

But though the psychiatrist had left, there was a positive legacy. The flashes of good health persisted. Unexpectedly, my mother talked of studying philosophy. She decided that she was going to apply for a place at university as a mature student. I was delighted when she was accepted. This was a new person, someone who managed to drive a car, spend hours on the phone, who could write, discuss, enjoy. The house was stacked with tomes heavy both in weight and content. She was coping, very much the mother I knew before we moved. I was thrilled. My life was transformed. Homework was returned with unexpected good marks. My house-captain smiled benignly when I pulled in commendations for the red team rather than minus points. I was rushing home instead of dreading my return to the prison. Every day held more promise. We could begin again. In my mind, everything was possible. Once my mother stopped vomiting, and ate like other people, we could be a family once more, maybe sit at the table together, entertain visitors, ask people in for coffee, ask friends after school, venture out. I was grateful for every day. She was positive, living and fighting for her existence. I never noticed whether my father was even in the house.

Then suddenly, like switching off the power, all the magic stopped. It was presaged by yelling and quarrels. When the shouts and tears started I pulled my hands tight over my ears, ran to my room and prayed that they would stop fighting. I was so afraid of the other life returning. At first, my mother put up a fight. She'd fold her lips together in defiance, eat something, throw up, take a pill and slam out of the door. And she kept going. I was so proud.

But that energy that burned and delivered a scent of happiness in our home like a kind of incense was not to last. She was breaking the rules. Their rules. The old Victorian formula of the stronger man watching over and controlling the invalid wife had been shrugged aside by a new vital woman. He harboured a whole cluster of resentments. She wasn't there to put out his slippers and bring in his tea. She had her own friends. She was popular, independent and happy. Her private life with strangers was secret, separate, another world he could not reach. My mother's new friends told her not to tolerate his moods and fights but to break the shackles and run away with me to another place, but she couldn't do it. Exhausted by the tantrums she surrendered and returned to bed. She juddered back into her old life like the last death throes of Violetta in Verdi's *La Traviata*. I heard my father's jealous anger and hysterical screams and suddenly the books, the conversations and the phone calls dissolved into the mists of memory.

Somehow because I had tasted the good, licked my fingers with the honey-sweet times, the shock of return to the narrowed space of bedroom, and lounge made up with sheets and pillows, was even more claustrophobic, more final in its inevitability.

Like a child who has broken one of his favourite toys and has been rebuked but refuses to apologise, I suspect my father secretly repented his violent actions. There was always an interlude of pleasantness after the big rows, like a rich orange sunset that follows a day of cloud-blackened thunder. Just days later he came home with sheaves of multi-coloured travel brochures under his arm. He threw them on to my mother's bed nearly injuring her with their weight.

'Go on then, you choose,' he said. 'Find a place to go. It'll do you more good than sitting around the bedroom with that bastard.'

My mother picked up the brochures, gazed at my father as if he had bestowed some great gift, and clutched them like treasures.

It gave them both a new project. My mother somehow managed to find the strength to slip into town with me to buy a few new clothes. I always hated those shopping trips. My mother worried that everyone was gawping and commenting on her thinness and I suppose they were. And I was fatter than the last time. Some of the shop girls were truly tactless: 'Look at you and your mother. She's so thin you'd think she would blow away in a puff of wind.' Yes, yes cliché, but how often I heard it coupled with, 'and, gosh, aren't you big? You wouldn't think that you were mother and daughter!' or 'Is it your father's side of the family you get your weight from?'

People were not so careful in those days as to what they said. We would be regarded as exhibits in a freak show. I wanted to plead with them to shut up. My life was tough enough.

Words hurt. Staring hurt. Ignorant gestures hurt, peppering me with pain. But we keep smiling, don't we? The fat happy people.

It never worried my father. He enjoyed being the ringmaster, the head of the herd. Suddenly resilient. Mr Tough. Our leader. He was happy to toss out one of his pragmatic sayings like, 'When he's finished looking, he'll look somewhere else.'

But that didn't help. I still hurt and so did my mother. Sometimes she was better at covering up the hurt than one very large teenage girl who, during her mid-teen years, felt that her elephantine size was set forever, and that she was doomed to be the fat lady and foil for the skinny one.

But plans for the holiday would progress. I'd be excited. We were going away on holiday. It would be wonderful to be a whole family together. And in those early years we coped. Just. The mission would be controlled by my father.

He believed he was a professional driver, and it was his job to take us through France to the Italian sun to stay for a couple of weeks before turning back. The car was always his choice of transport. We never became part of the fly and flop brigade. Oh, this was so much more challenging – more fun. Nightly he'd pour over vast maps that took up my homework space in the kitchen. He'd send away for brochures. In those days it was still a little extraordinary to take the car abroad and once there we would hoot and wave if we encountered another GB registration on the road. My father enjoyed a non-involved camaraderie. He never chatted or demonstrated that he needed any show of friendship from these people when they were stopped. No, a wave would suffice.

I hated every moment of every journey. I was always severely car sick and thus deemed a nuisance and my father's erratic use of the accelerator and brake did not improve my situation. He felt he was on a personal mission to correct the driving skills of all other motorists on his route by honking the horn and gesticulating with vast redundant arm signals, constantly forcing us into a state of high drama.

It didn't help either that the car was right hand drive, for often he would depend on my mother's opinion as to whether he was able to overtake. We suffered many near-misses and mini-rows would follow.

'You said it was alright! You nearly got us killed then.'

'Well, it was, he came up quickly,' or, 'I didn't see him…'

Sullen silences would follow, with my mother's head hung over a bowl of vomit and my father driving angrily as if he had been forced into a car to drive a gang of crazies around. In between being sick, my mother would try to smooth things over, pretend that we were still a happy group of people on holiday enjoying themselves, asking me if I wanted to sing a family song or whether I liked the countryside.

And Dad's routes were dipped in a fascination with death and war. He was spellbound by battlefields, so, just as he loved his war-films at home, we would journey for hours through acres of monotonous, hideously sad, tiny crosses.

The destination was always booked on the first night of our trip. But after that we'd, as Dad put it, 'Take pot luck.'

'Half the fun is to drive and then see some place you fancy and stay the night.'

But it was not fun. From three o'clock I used to worry that we would not find a place. All the good ones went early and my mother chose according to the look of the outside, from the paintwork and its upkeep to the beauty and abundance of the window boxes, while my father studied the Michelin Guide. If the Auberge or L'Hotel was blessed with two or three stars we were allowed to stop. Their two criteria would match so infrequently. If they did, then my mother would have to inspect the public toilets – if there were any – and the rooms. Sometimes she'd return disgusted and we would move on. It had to be the perfect place in the prettiest town and often it was not and we would drive until we were desperate and darkness was falling.

In the back of the car, my mind would be fraught with fears. Most focussed around my father's anger and its consequences. A disaster had to happen, and it did on one particular holiday.

Suddenly, a balmy French summer changed without warning into an electric storm. A stone from the road hit the windscreen and shattered it entirely. My father drove on relentlessly, and, as well as the torrential downpour that soaked our bodies, hundreds of flies and stinging creepy crawlies fell upon the speeding windscreen-less car. My mother screamed with terror. My father shouted at her: 'It's not so terrible – it's a few bloody flies!'

But from the first mosquito hitting her my mother was hysterical and the road's darkness seemed relentless. Eventually we discovered a very poor village inn. We were grateful to find anything. I'll never forget my mother's sobbing tears as I combed her hair, tangled with insects. I vowed at that moment that if I was ever independent, I would never tour in a car.

Other times were punctuated by events that should have been fun, like the shopping trips for picnics. As there were no cool bags in the late fifties, and food was often left in the car from the day before, it was my responsibility to constantly review the state of the brown bags and mouldering vegetables sitting on the back seat. My mother's enthusiasm for French food markets was unparalleled – she loved to see the displays of fruit, the tiny sliced-open Charantais melons, fragrant and bright orange inside, punnets of raspberries, wild strawberries and apricots. They bought French sticks and masses of different cheeses and delicatessen items. My father shared her passion for buying because he loved spending money on her. They'd always buy too much and the parcels would jostle for attention in the back of the car. Coming from their background of scarcity, it was an unwritten rule that we never threw anything away. So every day there was at least an hour's discussion on the state of the packages

'Mum, the melons have gone off.'

'Oh, they can't have, we only bought them two days ago.'

'Well, they've gone. They've got bits of mould on them.'

'Can't we cut the bad bits off?'

'And the Camembert – it's…'

(Father) 'Nothing wrong with that! I'll eat that, it's supposed to have a mould…'

'Yes, but…'

The French eat many strange foods enveloped in rich sauces and aspic. I tried to say no but my mother's great pleasure was choosing my food for me and for peace's sake I would allow her.

'Darling, try that… it looks lovely.'

So often I would eat a meal of something congealed and wrapped in pastry or clothed in a cold sauce. I never said that I didn't like it for to say anything would seem spoilt. I suspect my vegetarianism and passion for plain good food served in its simplest state was conceived on these trips.

All these foods had their own smells which were appealing when they were fresh, on a plate, with cutlery, at a table, with a cloth serviette and a chilled glass of wine. But left in a warm car overnight, their scent became that of an overwhelming compost heap, compounded by the stench of my poor mother's vomit, which hung about the car like the spirit of a demon squatter.

But there were infrequent good times. Times when we reached our destination early and explored tiny stone French villages surrounded by the mossy darkness of rivers. Small fairy-tale villages like Nougat, where the whole town smelt of toasted nuts and sweetness. Or Lyon, a buzzing, busy town where ornate figures of snails adorned each building. There were towering chateaux in the Loire with their feet dipped in moats of history, shouldered with turrets holding captured princesses and fairies. And sunlit afternoons of fresh, rich coffee and patisserie with my father and I eating the richest and gooeyest. My mother would be nibbling daintily on a Grissini or arrowroot biscuit from the car, hiding it under the table and sipping a lemon tea, whilst watching us and absorbing our reactions, in a kind of osmosis of pleasure.

'What's in it, Geoff?' she'd say. 'Let's see the middle.'

Dad would cut it and rave – 'Oh it's got chocolate, pureed apricots, crème patissiere,' or some other delicacy. And they'd enthuse together as if she had also tasted and eaten it. This seemed to trigger memories for them. They'd talk about their safer childhood memories, dipping into the sweetness of their past and licking their fingers.

Dad: 'Do you remember bienenstich?'

Mum: 'Oh, it was gorgeous. Us kids could never afford to have it because it came from very posh bakeries and you can't buy cake for nine kids. And it had to be kosher. But one of the maids once gave me a taste. I remember it was wonderful…'

'Mm. A rich soft cake – was it yeast or sponge?'

'I don't remember – I only remember the topping.'

'I think but I may be wrong but the proper way was a yeast cake layered with a rich custard and then another layer of sponge and then the topping …'

'Ah yes, the topping…'

'Slivers of toasted almonds shining in a buttery golden caramel set on top – crunchy, ooh!'

'And do you remember baumkuchen – we never had that either but we used to see huge ones in the bakeries when we walked past, on our way to school.'

'Gosh, I'd forgotten about those. But someone explained to me once how they did it. They used to have special machines to create the cakes, like a revolving spit, covered with paper, and the cake mixture was ladled over the paper several times whilst some was removed from time to time so that somehow lines of dark and light were created and a wood pattern evolved. Then when the cake was cool it was covered with apricot puree and chocolate or icing…'

'I wonder who invented it in the first place – who had the idea?'

'And then there's streusel kuchen covered with that buttery crumble and real rye bread and sachertorte and…'

Foods would be revered as the seeds of better times. Memories nurtured and fostered by a slice of cake. I loved those chats: the good times when my parents talked as a couple to each other, relating in friendly communication, under trees that listened to them while sculpting the light into freckled shapes.

But those moments were rare and happened only during a few early holidays. It's strange to remember how Mum and

I could take a gentle walk along white stony paths through orchards or sleepy lanes, her thin arm resting in mine, the sun hot on our backs. She'd talk to me, her face rapt and involved with the landscape.

'Darling, look how beautiful. Store this moment in your mind... Look at that clump of poppies.'

Then, in the middle of talking, she'd walk a few yards further, by a hedge or a ditch in the road, and deftly vomit her last meal, carefully wipe her mouth with a tissue, and return, as if that break in our conversation was nothing more than a comma in our lives.

At one stop I forgot to repack her plastic vomit bowl under the car seat. At the very next sign of habitation, we managed to find a house-ware shop with a French assistant who spoke English.

'We need a small bowl, please,' said my mother.

'Is it for mixing?' asked the French assistant.

'No, it's already mixed,' muttered my father.

We all thought that was hysterically funny and could hardly get out of the shop for laughing. That crazy, upside-down world of sickness had contorted our humour. Or maybe it was good to laugh at the horror, and confront its twisted face.

I was just fifteen and the year was 1961. We were going for a six week holiday in the car. I packed all the suitcases, all the pills, all the emergency foods, all the clothes. It was going to be a wonderful trip, a week travelling through France, a week returning, and four wonderful weeks in Italy in an apartment, sitting under fragrant pine-trees, sipping coffee and listening to the lap of soft blue waters on stony shores. I'd finished my own packing and lugged all the suitcases to the front door. Then I returned to my mother's bedroom. I knew something was wrong as I walked in – the putrid air told me – but I tried to pretend to myself that all was well. She was lying on the bed with a staring look in her eyes and her voice was husky and sore from vomiting.

'Don't tell Daddy!' she said. 'I feel awful.'

'Does that mean…?'

'No, no, we'll go. We've got to go. I'll be better when we get there. And anyway, we've so looked forward…'

She was grey as she climbed in the car. My father, always obsessed with perfect packing, had his head in the boot rearranging for the third time and missed the signs. Just twenty minutes away, outside Newport, Mum heaved over her orange plastic bowl, then lifted her body back and leaned hard against the car-leather for support. Her eyes were raised to the ceiling of the car as she fought off a fainting attack. Dad was furious.

'If you think we're bloody going with you in this state, you've got another think coming.'

Weakly my mother tried to speak – to protest. With a squeal of the car tyres my father turned the car, his shoulders swaying with fury as we sped home. All the time my mother was trying to speak, waving her thin hand in the air, as if that could form the words. I called the doctor, then unpacked the carefully washed and ironed clothes.

My exterior world was narrowing. But the dramas within our house expanded. And as an only child – the one in goal, piggy in the middle – I maintained my position in the only way I knew. I became my parent's stomach.

Chapter Seven

I Am My Parents' Stomach

The distortions in my parents' attitude to food had always been there but we skirted around them. It was like avoiding a tree-stump growing in the living room. All their wants, their needs, were expressed through food. My father had courted my mother during the war with presents of food: tins of fruit, kosher salami and chocolate. In the beginning of their relationship in Gateshead, they liked to offer each other special tit-bits to eat like birds courting in the nest. Later, when I arrived and there was still rationing, it was a challenge to my mother to provide her family with the most perfect, most nutritious, most substantial food she was able to. During this time, she felt valued, needed. Both my parents wanted to improve their place in society and my mother gained her friends through her ability to create the most delicious food. She was able to cook much better than her contemporaries. When I was a small child, my mother reproduced the Jerusalem Baby Home, out of cake, to auction. Apparently it was perfect. Sadly, no picture survives. It was decorated with tiny nappies made out of rice-paper, hung from a white cotton washing line on the flat sugar-icing roof, and the original surrounding trees and bushes copied to ornament the exterior. Although she died in 1971, that cake is still a legend in our community. So food and its preparation gave her position and status. But as time passed and my mother was unable to maintain her cooking ability, that talent twisted its ugly head and laughed at her. Gradually food the friend became a hypocrite. It promised with all its fragrances and associations to be a comrade, but behind our backs it was conspiring with sickness and death to mislead us.

As my father's absences became more frequent and longer, my mother rejected her food and begged me to taste. I became a surrogate stomach. I would come in from school usually starving and still exhausted from nursing her the night before and her first question would be, 'What are you going to have, love?'

Usually, my answer was vague – 'Oh, anything. I've got loads of homework so I can't really…'

But it would be to no avail. She had planned all day what she wanted me to prepare. If it was the beginning of the week and my father had just left, then she'd want to concoct something 'just for us'. Thursday and Friday would be spent preparing the goodies for my father's return.

'Oh, love, how do you fancy pancakes? Drop scones, mountains of toast spread with jam or honey, scrambled egg with mushrooms and cheese slices melted into the top?'

Or: 'Let's make something naughty,' she'd say, and I'd see a gleam in her eye. A glint of excitement. I had to foster that small light and keep it going.

Thin and ill as she was, she'd make her way into the kitchen hanging on to the worktops for support. I'd bring in her sick-bowl, pillows and an extra hollowed latex pillow, cut in a circle with a hole in the centre so that her poor bony behind could sit without pain. Then she'd sit at the little fifties diner she'd installed in the corner. With her head cupped in an embrace of bones, she'd make an effort to smile.

'This is fun, isn't it, darling?'

'Get the mixer out, let's make bread,' or 'get out the toastie machine, let's make toasted tasties.' I never argued. I wasn't a pathetic lump, even though it seems on reflection that I was. I was just grateful that she was able to be in the kitchen and enjoying something. To say no, and I did try it very occasionally, was to cause instant conflict. It was easier in my food-stacked prison to agree.

When the food was made she'd say: 'You sit where Daddy sits and eat there, and I'll watch you.'

And I'd sit opposite her and she'd watch, like a kind of eating voyeur, licking her thin tired lips, her mouth dry with exertion. There would be questions all the time.

'Is it nice? Should we have added anything else to it? Can you taste the vanilla, grated lemon?' And then, 'What else are we going to have?'

Eventually there is no more protest. The body starts to crave all these crazy foods. Soon, without encouragement, you are thinking about a pint of custard for tea, or dipping in the packet of the mixed dried fruit or helping yourself to bowls of cereal. And each day as you return from school, when maybe you've felt the pain of laughter when you have not been able to leap-frog over the horse, or scale a rope, or have had to stand in the showers with the slim, slim girls and feel your flesh wobbling as they hide their shocked and giggling faces, there has to be some comfort. Something to help the time pass. A reason to rush home and look forward. Inmates of prisons and institutions spend hours dreaming about food.

My parents would settle arguments with food. They would have perhaps rowed for hours. She had called him and he hadn't answered or she had heard suspicious voices on the phone when she had phoned him. They would yell at each other. Finally my mother would crave harmony. 'Anything for peace,' she'd say. Then she would call, 'Do you want coffee and cake, then, Geoff?'

If he acquiesced, they would be friends again.

As other couples made love, so my mother fed my father, but I was always included in the deal. No choice. If I said 'no' I was being difficult, showing contempt. Sometimes my father would bring food from town. If he walked past the bakery it would be two large coffee puffs the size of small elephant's feet each. Although I hated the cream, and always felt sick after and tried to protest, he still bought them. When he was at home and not on his travels, he fell into a habit of stopping at a bakery on the way to the house and arriving with food presents. My mother loved that moment. Sometimes she'd say, 'Let's have a taste, no, no, no – a tiny taste.' He'd break off a doll's portion and she'd roll it around her tongue, her eyes expressing the taste, savouring each flavour. I'd hope that it would stay there but, when she'd had an eighth of a teaspoon full of macaroon or marzipan or chocolate, she spend the rest of the evening vomiting it away.

My father didn't only bring cake home. There is a passage in my life that fills me with embarrassment. I still blush with my own stupidity. But, at the time, whatever my father brought home to eat, I ate. I trusted him. In that respect I was still very much a child. Indeed, whatever my father or my mother did, I trusted. I never for one moment thought that I shouldn't. Does that make me a fool? Maybe. Dad knew that we were orthodox Jews who followed the rules of *kashrut*. My mother took great trouble as a chief rabbi's daughter to ensure that the food that came into our house was kosher. And all our dishes and utensils were deemed kosher. I'm sure Dad began his strange purchasing habits with an idea of pleasing my mother. She was ill and fancied calves'-foot jelly and as a Jewish family that was impossible for us to source. One day he came home with a calf's foot which he said had come from our kosher butcher. I just unpacked it, though at the time, for a few seconds, I wondered why it was wrapped in newspaper, rather than the brown paper wrapping of the kosher butcher. But I popped it in the koshering bucket, topped it up with water to soak and remove the blood, then laid it on the wooden slats and salted it, like any other piece of meat. When it was 'koshered' I simmered it gently, with carrots, onions and celery. I gave some of the broth to my mother and cut the rest into small pieces whilst simmering the broth even further until it naturally formed a jelly. She ate it all. I fed it to her. Similarly, my father began to bring home various cold cuts from a delicatessen. As I never visited the butcher and again trusted my father, I assumed that these cuts were kosher. We all ate them, particularly on the Sabbath, on the festival challa bread. Years later, when I had a home of my own, I walked into a local delicatessen asking for a clear red blancmange-type pudding mix called rote groetse which I used to adore. The owner of the deli asked me why I never came in for the ham sausage my father always bought. Didn't I like it anymore? I will never forget the shock, the hideous discomfort as this man gently teased me. My mother and I had been betrayed.

The habits of fat slipped gently about my hips and thighs so that I gained a stone with each year. Twelve stone at twelve. Thirteen stone at thirteen. Fourteen stone at fourteen. I laughed. I was jolly. I made jokes at the back of the class, covered my mouth and giggled, to mask the fact I had not managed to do the homework. I was loud. I was the fat girl in school. I waddled on to the games field and tried. But I was never included. The exception was the hockey team. My bulk provided the first team with an intimidating sight for the opposition after the bulky pads were belted on, as I stood rigid in goal. Hockey was my only bond with that school world and the hockey teacher, an ex Welsh international, the only teacher in the school who ever offered a few words of sympathy, who understood a little of my home life. I was grateful for her friendship. But when my mother discovered that there was someone in the school who was kind to me, she became incensed with jealous fury. That was hard to bear. So I never mentioned the teacher at home.

My fatness became my excuse not to join in activities. Rather than admit my parents' protests, it became the reason for saying 'No', 'Sorry', 'I wish I could'. I had to look after my mother so I could not – was not allowed to – stay after school for drama club, fencing, tennis – the fun things others considered their right. And meeting socially after school, discos, parties, never. And as I matured, this mantle of obligation enveloped my body with the corresponding pounds of blubber and told me that I did not have the right to be like the others.

We had our routine. I cooked the meals, emptied sick-bowls and escaped to the kitchen to do my homework – if there was any time left – working in the kitchen at the little diner with the sound of the television in the other room. A few times, I tried to work in my room, but without a desk and only a bed it was too difficult and I hated a space without music. So the sounds of laughter on a television in another room became my other life, the life I might join after I had finished with my books. Late at night, I'd listen to Radio Luxembourg under the bedclothes: my clandestine connection with another world, a forbidden existence. In my parents' eyes all these people were drug-takers and perverts. But I loved the DJs and pretended I was part of a funky sixties reality and when the truth became too tough, which was frequent, I escaped in my mind to this other existence where people partied all night, wore extraordinary clothes and made love. Oh yes, they always made love.

But things were changing again, slipping up a gear. Now, if I did show any resentment toward my own situation, I paid. Mum became more ill and penalties were applied. A noose tightened around my space.

Very occasionally, I asked to go out. The replies were swift, accusing.

'Why? Do you have to? So what is so special about this person – these people?'

'Nothing, Mum, I'd just love to go out once…It's only the Kardoma for a coffee…please?'

I'd look at their faces, pleading silently with my father who would have the job of watching her for those few hours. There was no point in considering a coffee if he was away.

'Please, just for an hour or two?'

Then the questions would start: 'Is it necessary?' 'Do you really think…?' 'In the middle of the week!' 'Why is this person more important than us?' 'Is your homework finished?'

My answers would peter out in this barrage of cross-questioning.

Then, their final objection would be connected with food. 'But we were going to have the casserole…' the meatballs. Food, it was suggested, that would go off if it was not consumed that night.

I'd watch the thin face begin to hyperventilate and my father's face scowl. Weakly I'd scan my mother's expression.

'Oh, alright, I won't go, I'll phone Carolyn or Barbara.'

But it never finished there. My mother would continue.

'You wanted to leave me. There was someone more important than me to see.'

'No, Mum, It was only for a couple of hours – a little break…'

'Oh yes, you need a break from me, I'm such a nuisance to you.'

'No, Mum, you're not…I'll make the phone call now.'

At this point, my father would slope off; have his hour in the toilet with a Raymond Chandler paper-back, followed by a full evening's bath and manicure in his bedroom. In the summer, he'd escape to the greenhouse to lavish his male love on tiny cuttings of fuchsias, African violets, and geraniums that he grew from seed. The drama had ended. My mother would most probably be a little sicker that evening and I would bear the guilt. I asked less and less.

Food was our family's obsession. The discussion of food, the preparation of food, the serving of food, always with the correct crockery or utensils, a butter knife, a milk jug, a butter dish to hold one or two tiny pats. And when the food was finished, the left-overs had to be saved. It would be placed in smaller dishes to be used at the next meal, this going into yet smaller dishes, and never discarded. And then the whole eating ceremony. Food was pushed on a trolley in front of my father. He ate it – I ate it – as if partaking in an ancient ritual, chewing words of discussion, a kind of dialogue to its tenderness, leanness, and difficulty of purchase. Gargantuan portions of meat in gravy would be poured over pasta, rice and mashed potatoes, whole fish grilled and served with sauté potatoes, and massive apple pies drenched with lemon juice, sugar and layered with sultanas and mixed spices.

My mother would hover – and even if I'd followed the recipe by rote, she would ask, a second before serving, to taste. I've watched her take the wooden gravy spoon in shaking thin hands and with a tired dry tongue lick a morsel off the bowl.

'Needs a tiny bit more salt,' or, 'Add a drop of *Kiddush* (holy fortified wine) to the mixture' or, 'needs more mushrooms'. Then she'd almost fall and I'd help her back to her seat and start preparing her menu.

It is difficult to remember what I prepared for her meals, as if those miniscule amounts have faded in my mind to nothing at all. A world of tiny atoms passed through a needy pair of lips: fingers of toast, crackers high-baked and broken into mouse-sized mouthfuls, morning coffee biscuits broken into six, counted on the plate, tiny pieces of steamed chicken eaten hungrily and then so often lost down the toilet pan hours later.

My mother was wasting and disappearing before us.

As I grew, encouraged by my parents' appetites, my clothes became tighter. There was little opportunity to go shopping. I had no money. Anyway getting clothes my size would have been difficult.

Now it seems so ironic. My father was in the clothing trade, handling hundreds of garments every week, and yet I had so little to wear. He even stocked an outsize range that might have been suitable, but he wouldn't buy them for me. And it was a time of clothes. A wave of fashion for the new 'teenage' market was sweeping the country. We were no longer following our parents' tastes, but had our own styles. My parents' financial priorities were restricted to expensive suits for my father, the smartest car he could drive that was not German (these were considered essentials for work), kitchen equipment to prepare food, food and more food, books and more books, and plants for the garden.

I would try to pluck up the courage to ask for clothes forced, maybe, by the pop of buttons or a weal that would appear after a metal zip had ground its way into my body. I knew an argument would result.

'Are you suggesting for one moment that I do not provide you with enough clothes?'

'I didn't say that.'

'What exactly did you say?'

'I just wondered... well, thought...'

'Yes?'

'Well, my clothes are getting tighter and I just wondered if I could get...?'

'What's wrong with that blue dress... that red...'

'Daddy, I've had that a year!'

'You think I'm made of money? Can't you let out the seams? You've only just had for Yomtov. I only just bought you a pair of shoes.'

'No, school shoes...I had to have.'

'Yes, that's the trouble with you. You've always got to have...'

'Yes, but…'

It was hopeless. No point. Better to keep silent and reassemble a shapeless conglomeration of jumpers and blouses and dream of one day casting my blubber away, leaving revealed an elegant, slim and attractive woman. So I read the papers, collected pictures of elegant clothes from my mother's discarded magazines and just hoped that one day I would design my own.

The only escape for me was on a Sunday morning, when, legitimately, I was able to be part of another world. I attended the teen version of Hebrew classes. I must have been the only person in the Jewish teen world who actually looked forward to and enjoyed going to *Chaeder*. My mother never argued, as the classes were in keeping with her religious ideals. Most of the Jewish girls regarded that morning as a chance to talk over the parties from the night before. To me it was just out. Blessed freedom.

After the class, at twelve-thirty precisely, my father would be waiting outside the synagogue in his car to take me home. I wanted to walk with the others. Tell stupid jokes, coo over one of the girls' new tops – be part of the gang. Luckily, I never resented other people's lives. I am fortunate to be blessed with a non-envious personality. I just wished that my workload was less. You'd have thought that any normal human being in my situation would have felt some resentment. But I can only believe that my fatness helped me somehow create my own barrier against envy. What would have been the point, anyway? Nothing was going to change. I wore my brooch of devotion, the good daughter, the reliable one. The one who was always there.

Chapter Eight

Pretending the Bad Days Away

What I feared, during my latter years in school, what I dreaded, were 'the bad days'. They would be presaged, if my father was in Cardiff, by his arrival at school. He'd drive into the reserved parking places and a screech of tyres would announce the car's positioning next to the headmistress's car. This was strictly forbidden and those girls able to watch out of the windows would stare and mutter to each other that some idiot person had broken the rules. The whispers circulated that a stranger was pacing through the headmistress's entrance, also strictly forbidden. Even visiting without an appointment was not allowed. Now, these rules seem strange, but we are talking about a grammar school in the sixties and a girls' school with very high standards of discipline.

He'd march through the building. I'd hear the polished leather shoes on the shining block-wood floor, seconds before the door was flung open. He'd stride in and stare around, not bothering to apologise to the teacher. I was always huddled at the back, the other girls would be giggling, and without a further word or some kind of courtesy, he'd shout: 'Ruth, your mother needs you! Now...! Move...!'

His eyes would blaze with a mixture of fear and anger and I'd hear a titter of subdued laughter from covered mouths rippling around the class. Reluctantly, I'd pull myself out of the chair; feeling my face rise to red as he yelled again: 'Well, come on...She's bad...Get a move-on...' And I'd leave, to the astonishment of whichever teacher had had her class interrupted by this ignorant man. I felt her opinion of him, stick like a label on my back, to add to the fat label, and the lazy-doesn't-bother-with-homework label.

I would return home, always fearful of what I would find. More likely than not the following days would be spent emptying sick-bowls, bedpans, and trying, cajoling, persuading, my mother to eat something. Anything.

We'd run through the thin menu.

'Would you like some soup – I'll make it with a skinned chicken breast and you need only have the liquid – I'll take every bit of fat off? I promise.'

'No…It's too rich!'

'Well, will you have a bit of mashed potato made with water, or a small bowl of porridge, the thinnest of toast –?'

'No, no, I can't have toast. My throat is so sore from being sick.'

'But Mummy, you've got to have something, please eat something. Otherwise you'll end up in hospital again.'

Sometimes with that threat sitting like a gargoyle above her head, and her own knowledge of the severity of her illness, I was able to pull her back from the edge and persuade her to eat. But often I couldn't. Often she would be severely ill.

I would have to prepare my special recipe to bring her back from semi-consciousness, by liquidising tinned peaches thickened with a little arrowroot and a teaspoon of honey. Then I'd sit at the side of her bed and plead, to the tiny face, hollowed into the pillow.

'Come on, love, you've got to take this…'

And I'd lift her head and try to slip a teaspoon of the slippery liquid past her lips. It would be our last chance. If that didn't work I'd be crouched in the back of a clanging ambulance again. Then, with or without my father, I'd be hunched outside a ward, in a corridor gloss-painted in green or mushroom with a shiny lino floor that smelt of disinfectant and malady, while behind jolly flowery screens the medical staff forced my mother back to life with plastic tubes and wires.

So many times that happened. As she became worse the treatments became more drastic. The registrars would stare at my mother, the 'interesting case', and bring in their students to prod and question and discuss over her the next form of cure and the only course of action. Early on it was described as ulcerative colitis, later as a form of hysteria. My father would be taken into a room and I would wait for news. Sometimes she was sent to hospitals in other parts of the country where under the leadership of some new brilliant, guru-esque consultant she would be treated with some new radical idea. Each time we hoped. She was dispatched to St Thomas's Hospital in London. Someone had suggested she was suffering from Anorexia Nervosa. They used massive doses of drugs called Largactil, knowing they caused acute symptoms of hunger. They also cause hunger pains and hallucinations. Given her fragile mental state at the best of times, there could be no success. She phoned me desperately, telling me to tell my father to get her out of there. At another hospital in Highgate, where she lay for months, she became a different person. Quiet, docile, drugged. My father paid for her stay. The penultimate consultant, Harley Street of course, suggested a lobotomy, which the Concise Oxford Dictionary describes as 'a surgical operation involving an incision into the prefrontal lobe of the brain formerly used to treat mental illness.'

The final consultant suggested a process where they would just save her head, and freeze it – cryonics. That was when we lost belief in them. We'd touched hope but it slipped out of our grasp. Is Anorexia Nervosa just a mental illness, or is it a combination of predisposition, past history, ancient agonies? Is it peculiar to a personality type – the type that demands perfection and insists on the highest level of success? Certainly it's influenced by the attitudes of peers –

109

the curious admiration of the thinning shape that can be perfected by control. In the sixties, cases of Anorexia were far less evident than today and little known to the average doctor.

What I hated about those dark days were the empty-shelled promises. Promises for a cure: that all would be made better. When our fragile hopes were dashed, and the consultants had moved to their next interesting case, they were not the ones to carry home the pieces.

It was 1963, I was seventeen and it was as if someone flicked off the light. We stumbled in the darkness of my mother's and our own despair. Now my father and I could walk into the house at any time and my mother would be sitting in the large chair in the lounge banging her belly like a drum to remove the food that she said hurt her. The house that had been her dream home had turned into a casing of ugly smells. The odours of vomit and the results of laxative misuse hung about the air. No one except a few loyal friends visited any more.

Mental escape kept me sane. It gave me something to haul myself out of bed for in the morning and still wear a bright smile. My imagination became my friend, and day-dreams made my life bearable. I pretended I had a boy friend. How would I manage to meet a boy, let alone go out on dates, have a social life? It was impossible. Partying girls were myths and legends to me. I'd been to the occasional event when someone felt sorry for me, or their parents had said that I should be invited. But as I had a curfew imposed by my father of ten thirty, even at weekends (eleven o'clock after the age of twenty), I missed most of the action.

I'd witnessed the others snogging in corners, dark shadowed figures with their mouths tasting and anxious fingers fumbling. Somehow, though, I managed to stay disconnected. Now I cannot comprehend how I managed to disassociate myself from the sweet mouthings that surrounded me. But I was able to keep sane and remain detached. I lived in my world of pretend and befriended the girls that nobody wanted, for nobody wanted my body.

My imaginary boyfriend was a special man who was an amalgam of the beautiful males postered to my bedroom wall. There was Richard Greene as Robin Hood who charmed Maid Marion with a British toothy charm and rescued her constantly. The idea of someone to climb up rampart walls and take me from my tower to a place of beauty was particularly attractive. And there was Ben Casey – the vast, strong, male doctor with a good body who also had a kind demeanour. And was I looking for 'kind'?

At school, I was preparing for my A levels. My class mates were sending for university prospectuses from all over the country. I did the same. My father managed to attend a parent/students' careers evening to discuss my future. After the evening, I talked to my mother and father and said that I wanted to go to university and that I would apply to Cardiff as my first choice, but that I would also like to apply to Reading and Exeter who both ran the Sociology course that interested me. They gave me their blessing. Cardiff became my first choice. It seemed logical and sensible. I would be able to study, but still care for my mother.

By now, my mother was no longer venturing outside the house, but held the fragile threads of her world together by talking to friends on the phone. And every day, out of an overdeveloped sense of duty, she would begin by ringing my grandmother, even though they had never cared for each other. This grandmother, whom my parents had escaped from in Gateshead, had finally – much to my mother's horror – followed her son to Cardiff. She now lived with her husband in a house close by. But the relationship hadn't improved – it was always needled with splinters of resentment on both sides. My mother had craved substitute parents – desperately needing love – but my grandmother was a hard woman who had fought every day for her survival and her possessions and still hated the fact that her son had married a religious penniless woman like my mother.

I never realised the extent of my grandmother's feelings towards my mother, until one day when my mother was desperately ill. I was at home – the storming raid to haul me out of school had happened a week ago. Both my father and I were sitting at her bed-side and I was crying, terrified – was my mother dying? I was stroking her hand, her fingers tipped with those elegantly perfect nails, and chasing recipes through my mind to find some new concoction that might bring her back from the brink.

The doorbell rang: special messenger. A small package to be delivered to my mother from my grandmother.

I ran upstairs carrying the package

'Grandma's sent you a parcel, Mummy.'

A faint light shone in my mother's eyes.

'Oh, how lovely, Geoff, Geoff, see what it is…'

My father untied the string and unwrapped the brown paper layer to reveal a small cardboard box. He prised open the lid. Inside was a layer of cotton wool. He removed the cotton wool and he lifted out a small porcelain ornament. For seconds we could not discern a shape, but once out –

My mother continued asking, repeating and repeating 'What is it Geoff? What is it?

His face crumpled and looked grey and shadowy. 'It's a…'

'Let me hold it…please…but…but…it's a coffin!'

Hours later my mother was admitted to hospital. My father never confronted his mother about her 'gift'.

The 'A'levels I was taking were English and History. (I did want to add Art but my parents would not permit that. Art was my mother's talent). However, in order to reach the high-quality standards of a good sixth-form essay, it was necessary to seek other reference books and time at the library was essential. It was very hard to escape but when my mother was in hospital or when she was in bed in the morning, I sneaked away for a few hours.

So there were odd moments when I sat with a mound of books in the sweet whispered silence of the Cardiff Old Library. Large windows set into the old stone building were kept open most of the time. Breezes blew over pen-chewing, head-scratching students while the reverential push of ladders by dedicated librarians scraped gently across the floor.

It was there I discovered the power of flirting. I was grossly overweight, but sitting down most of that bulk disappeared. My hair was long and curly, falling over my shoulders, and my eyes were good and there always seemed to be someone who would murmur, or pass a folded note across a desk space. These were not make-believe people, but real flesh and blood; people who were interested in me. That frisson – that exchange of looks, a flash of eye-lashes, smiles returned, a coffee stolen at the Argosy Cafe and an occasional phone call to my home quickly ended by my father – left me with the excitement of knowing that I could be attractive and that there was a wonderful world out there. That perhaps I could find my way out of the tunnel, somehow.

But exams loomed – and my future depended on my grades. On the eve of my 'A' levels, I began to develop pains in my stomach. As I always suffered from severe period pains, my mother assumed that was the reason. She was angry with my moans and told me not to make such a fuss. Between gasps, I told her to call the doctor. Once again she was resentful, but she did it. Our faithful doctor came within the hour, and called an ambulance. It was discovered that my appendix had burst and that I had peritonitis. After surgery, I was taken back to the ward. A mixed surgical ward. Although I'd had a general anaesthetic, and many stitches, I still took my A levels the next day, with an invigilator sitting at the end of the bed, watching in case I had stowed a reference book. Then I had a week of recuperation with strangers. I must have seemed very odd, for when it came to leave, I sobbed. Despite the pain I had enjoyed my stay. I'd tasted another world of light food, newspapers and easy banter, a whole week without rows and with people who wanted my company, just for friendship.

Predictably my results were disappointing: a D and an E. My father delightedly called me a dope. My fate was decided, I thought. I left school with the others and said goodbye to a kind of security. We cried, even though we had all pretended that we were desperate to leave. We promised to keep in touch. However most of the other girls had mentally packed up their lives and moved on.

But then, to my greatest surprise, two crisply printed letters with delicious wording arrived addressed to me from Exeter University and Reading University, offering places if I still wished to take them.

'Mummy, I can still go, Daddy…they still want me…either Reading or Exeter, they still…'

I gazed at their expressions. They did not mirror my happiness. My mother began to breathe fast and my father slowly stubbed out a cigar.

'Well, Ruth, if you have to go, you go.'

'But I thought you promised…you understood…I –'

'Yes, you just go and enjoy your life and your friends – they are obviously more important than us.'

'It's not that…I wanted…'

'Yes, it has to be what you want…'

'But I…'

'They've always been more important – the other people in your life…'

'But it's my chance to make something of myself…'

'Yes, fine, you go just go but remember there will be no one to look after your mother.'

Stupid, stupid girl. I ran upstairs to my yellow and black bedroom, fell on the bed and sobbed for hours. But my tears were wasted. No one came and smoothed my head and told me that everything would be better, or that things would change. I'd cried like that before. I should have been used to broken promises.

A couple of hours later, I came downstairs, cleared the debris from my father's supper on the trolley, washed the dishes and cut myself an enormous slice of cake. I tasted nothing. But I ate it all the same.

That night, I contemplated leaving home, just opening the door to my prison and slamming the old life behind me. But I had no money, not even my own bank account, as my father would not allow it, and I was sensible enough to realise that a certain amount of money was necessary to start a new life. And, despite the broken promises, I loved my parents and especially adored my mother. So I did nothing.

The next day it was still a war-zone in the house with my parents on the offensive in case I signed up for university in their absence. I went to a phone-box and spoke to a few friends from school but they were so excited at the prospect of their own futures that they could hardly consider my situation. And somehow, in the shadowy recesses of my mind, I had known that all those dreams of university were make-believe.

My father and mother discussed my situation in my absence. My father, without talking to me first, spoke to the managing director of our local store who said there was a job as an accounts clerk within the store. I am totally innumerate. So in the summer of 1964, after leaving school at the age of eighteen, I was given the mammoth job of balancing the total of all the till rolls with the total takings of the store. There were no computers and not even a calculator – an entire mental arithmetic exercise. I never balanced. However, although the work was boring and impossible to manage, I gained. Other people were friendly. Meeting them in a non-school environment persuaded me to begin my silent revolution against the compulsory home-feeding sessions.

And perhaps it was by way of an apology that my father brought me home a dress. The largest he had in stock. It was a forty-six hip in royal blue with swathes of beige and green flowers. I hated it but it was my only choice. It was too tight and as I tried to pull it over my oversized hips, something inside me snapped forever. The flexible rubber person that was me screamed, enough! I would diet. My life would change from that moment. I began the process secretly and silently, trying all the short-cuts first, watching my mother – the mistress of starvation. I started drinking smelly soups concocted out of cabbage and water. Skipped meals at home and told them I'd eaten and then gnawed on carrot sticks. I pounded the water in the local pool in my lunch-hour and managed with a tiny bag of peanuts although I was starving. I drank gallons of black coffee at home, for I'd read somewhere that coffee stimulated the metabolism, and then bopped and twisted to the crazy beat of the caffeine, in the tiny confines of my bedroom. The fourteen and a half stone wobble became a thirteen and then a twelve. Suddenly, I had a waist and hips. I had to have more new clothes.

At last I was gaining some control over my life, and they could do nothing about it. A slightly less co-operative animal began to live in that house. I began to say no, just a little, beginning with food. I never felt angry but there must have been a new beast growing within me. I insisted that I went out. They agreed to once a week. I was eighteen years old and some of my friends were married. I needed to see people, make a few friends and my parents agreed, provided the company was Jewish. So I joined a religious study group. My parents never knew that I was the only girl. The boys there, I think, saw me as another bloke, but during discussions it was decided that a new charity group should be formed and I volunteered for the post of vice-chairman. I think I was elected because no one else wanted the work.

My chance had arrived. I was in reach of a social life. Meetings were planned and the first interfunction – that is, with other Jewish people all over the country – was scheduled for Droitwich, outside Birmingham, in a large house which could be hired in its entirety. My parents must say 'yes'. Everyone was going. By phone and letters I arranged the accommodation for our whole group, and planned all the catering. I enjoyed the bright buzz of choosing and buying clothes. I spoke of the arrangements many times at home though my parents always seemed distracted by their usual food-obsessed routines.

Two weeks to go and everyone was booked in a room except me. Deposits were needed. I would have to speak seriously to my parents. At the time my mother was averagely bad – what was that? Sick? Yes. Looking after her through the night? Yes. I was still living with the fetid smells of vomit and diarrhoea and desperately trying to be patient, loving, but at the same time listening to the noise of people beyond and wanting to climb on the merry-go-round of the world outside my house. I wanted to wear the clothes, stay out evenings, play.

I dreaded the moment. But I'd planned everyone's lifts, including my own.

'Mummy, you know how I've been organising Droitwich? Well, it's at the end of next week and I so want…'

'Impossible.'

'But…'

'Impossible, your father may be away…'

'But he makes appointments, he knows when…'

'Are you implying?'

Droitwich, apparently, was wonderful. I was used to disappointment. And in fact it somehow reinforced my resolve. I made friends, went to the odd party and continued to say no to food.

After an evening out, my mother would still want me to eat my pint of custard in front of her. She was still the needy voyeur. So that rich, creamy bowl of vanilla eaten at eleven pm, registering three hundred to three hundred and fifty calories on the slimming Richter scale, became my only meal for that day, apart from a few carefully spaced out apples and coffees, sandwiched between lies about massive meals. Lies became routine. I'd eaten before, I would eat later. I'd learnt from the mistress. And at parties I was too excited to think of food. It was people that mattered. Companionship I craved – not food. Sitting in the semi-dark with the throb of rock thrumming in my ears and a guy at my side. Although I was termed a 'big girl', I was usually with someone.

I loved the dancing best. Not the jiving or the twist, but the slow smooch – the feeling of a male body, up close. Firm hands, the scent of aftershave. But that was all. No one touched me otherwise. Nice girls didn't. The last thing I needed was an unwanted pregnancy – it was 1963. My girlfriends and I never contemplated sex before marriage, although it was discussed for hours in coffee bars within tight groups of teddy-boy hair-slicked lads and pony-tailed girls. Maybe they did it in London, but not in our small provincial Jewish universe.

Now determined to achieve and gain some credits in further education, I pleaded to go to college. Without consultation, my father enrolled me at the local business college – the College of Commerce. He walked into the house, threw a prospectus at me and bellowed, 'You're going to the local business college to do a Diploma in Business Studies in September. I've sorted it out.' I was shocked. But I didn't argue. I was programmed to be silent. I wanted to shout – 'But Dad, I have no interest in business at all. It's not for me. Look at all the trouble I had totting up all those figures. I am not a business woman. I want to study art.'

But I did not. I picked up the prospectus and placed it on the kitchen table while I prepared supper. The next morning after an easy night of nursing, I let myself silently out of the back door into his precious garden. The early morning sun was hot on my back. I watched heavy bumble bees land on the spotted throats of the foxgloves that had been lovingly planted by my father. I picked flowers for the vases that stood about the house. My mother insisted on four or five arrangements and I changed them twice weekly.

That morning, as I picked, my thoughts jumbled around in my head. I knew protests always caused a row and there seemed very little point in forcing the issue. 'I'll be out of the house for some of the time,' I reasoned to myself, 'and anywhere is better than being continually locked in, or that no-hope job.'

So in the autumn of 1964, I began an HND in Business Studies. We were a motley group of lads and two girls. I swiftly added 'A' level economics, accountancy, and law to my list of studies to prove to my father that I was not a dope. My first essay on the history of commerce came back with maximum marks and a note to see the teacher. I wondered why? He seemed a friendly man who sat on the front of his desk to show he was one of us.

'Look Ruth, I've studied this work – being blunt…'

'Yes?'

'Well, it's too good for us…you should be in university reading history or something…not stuck here. Look, there's still time – I could…'

'It's hopeless.'

I explained the position, but somewhere inside me, a small bird sang with joy. I was, anyway, starting to enjoy myself. There were mini packets of peanuts at the Cow and Snuffers, and laughs and coffees and the admiration of an Indian fellow student. The weight slipped off. I found a stack of slimming books from America that my mother had bought over the years and I began to study them in my room. They became my new hobby. There was one in particular, *The Reducing Cook-Book and Diet Guide,* first written in 1953, which was illustrated with small cartoon pictures of fat ladies trying to do up their zips while in the background a pig is laughing. Beside them is a slim elegant lady wearing high-heeled shoes and a pencil-slim skirt! I wanted to be that woman.

Fate played into my hands. My father had consulted his insurance company and he was told to lose weight. For a few days he was so angry. I watched him stare in the mirror pulling at his paunch. My mother protested: 'You've always been a big man, Geoff.'

But he was fearful. His father had died of a heart attack, and he realised that his feasting days were over. *The Reducing Cook Book and Diet Guide* became the family bible. We tried some dreadful concoctions of cold vegetables set into tomato jelly. We had to use kosher jelly, as the ordinary jelly was made with gelatine and that came from animal bones. The kosher jelly is created from carrageen and has a different texture and it would sit in the mouth like another form of life – immovable. We only had that a few times. But we were stewing apples and blackberries and pouring them into tall glasses and whisking mousses made with egg-whites and lemons instead of making cakes. We dumped the dumplings and the mounds of noodles for masses of cooked vegetables and grated salads made with carrots, cucumbers and pickled cucumbers, though my father hated them and rumbled about 'rabbit food' under his breath.

I stood on the scales and watched that glorious needle sliding down. One stone, one and a half stone, two stone and my clothes were loose. I would sit at my mother's sewing machine, under her very possessive eye, taking in vast seams in my clothes. My legs no longer rubbed together and the scars from chafing thighs were healing, while the weals those horrific fitted corsets had left on me were now all in the past. I could wear an ordinary bra – much to my mother's disgust. She felt it signified the beginning of my moral decline.

But I'd talked to friends and no one wore corsets any more. I can remember my father being furious at the waste of money. My mother was angry. Her words were stained with disgust.

'But you wobble – it looks disgusting!'

'I don't care…'

'Well, if you don't care, why should I worry? After all my efforts to drag myself there and get you the best.' I knew I'd pay: she'd be extra ill that night.

'If you want everybody to laugh at you wobbling, why should I worry?'

'But I'm not so bad now I've lost…'

Sometimes her words would haunt me in the night. My sleep, when I managed to get it, was punctuated by nightmares. These lasted well into my thirties. I would find myself in a boggy marsh up to my ankles in slime trying to speak but unable to. Or on a beach in winter shouting into an icy wind, my words freezing like pebbles rattling on a beach, as the sea tosses and grinds them. Or at the edge of a chasm with an imperceptible force pushing me closer and closer. I would be trying to scream. Or falling, falling down flights of stairs, to land with a shriek in a small basement where a light bulb swung on its flex. And then waking and shaking.

But I was older and slimmer and it was 1964. I had my college work and my night a week at the charity evening, with an occasional party to keep me quietly simmering. Now I had a girl friend from college who would swim with me when we could and share my peanut craze and encourage my weight-loss. I was beginning to have another life. I began to meet and enjoy the company of boys and I found some of them passably attractive. In the beginning, I thought if I engaged my parents' approval, I would have a smoother run. So I used to invite them to our house. I went out with one boy, who seemed pleasant. We talked politics and went to the theatre and shook hands at the end of the evening. But my father baited him with cruel jokes about his appearance. The next time, as I sat waiting to go out, with my body glamorously scented with a Goya bath-cube and fabulous pink Camay, and my hair set with an Amami wave set and conditioner and combed into a glorious beehive, he phoned. He was sorry but his mother said that he could not come out because his socks weren't aired. I wasn't surprised. There was only so much people could take of my father's taunting.

My mother started to select boys she thought were suitable for me. The lads were often her friends' children or else there was a religious connection which would make the match appropriate. The trouble was I found most of them boring. Polite, maybe, but boring. However, I let her continue to choose as the whole dating process seemed to me more about the preparation than the event itself. The anticipation, the washing and setting of hair the night before, the sweet torture of sleeping in rollers as I didn't have a hair dryer – my parents thought that far too self-indulgent. Then, on the day itself, a long bath and the decisions about the few clothes that fitted. All to the delicious music from my small radio.

The date that followed was often a battle of wills. He wanting to 'go all the way' and me stopping him getting to 'first base'. Like the majority of girls of that age, the fear of an unwanted pregnancy was my prime anxiety. I remember one boy I adored, who played the guitar and rode a motor bike, which seemed a mark of rebellion in itself. But he spent most of our time together wrestling with me on the floor, he like an explorer battling through the undergrowth of crimplene and bri-nylon to reach the promised land. He never did.

122

But everything changed on Christmas day 1965. We had organised a large charity interfunction weekend and people were coming from all over the country for meetings, parties and more parties. Most of the girls were having visitors to stay in their houses. I didn't even bother to ask. (Years before, a friend, who didn't know, had arrived at my door, and bounced in, friendly and cheerful. She saw my mother – the tiny clawing semi-cadaver – throwing up into a plastic bowl. She was so terrified of what she'd witnessed, she'd related the details to her mother. She was forbidden to see me again and especially never be my friend. After all, it could be catching.)

On this occasion, the first evening of the weekend, the chairman of the group had asked me to be his date. My mother considered him suitable as she was friends with his aunt and I was used to popping into his family home. I thought of him as tagged with a 'he'll do for the evening' label, not in any serious way. It was just wonderful to go out with someone and not have to spend hours justifying the reason or recounting their pedigree.

In fact this date seemed to be the culmination of all my mother's dreams. She was excited and persuaded my father to find me a dress from stock. For the first time in my life, my father brought me home a glorious dress in a normal size. A high-necked, sleeveless, gold lamé mini with a fashionable keyhole cut into the cleavage. I thought it was beautiful and because my mother was so impressed with the potential of my date, I was allowed to buy gold sandals to match.

I was left in peace to take a long bath and get ready and when I was dressed in my new outfit, I felt good for the first time. The bell rang – my date was punctual. My parents nodded their approval. We seemed to be in agreement. Everything was perfect.

'Darling, have a lovely time,' my mother called from the chair.

'Yes, go and…' my father said, almost pleasantly.

I opened the door and my escort stood outside, smartly dressed in a suit. He didn't acknowledge my looks at all but I wasn't used to compliments and didn't miss them. I was still euphoric. I followed the heavy dose of aftershave down the winding stone pathway to the garden gate and out. In the car, a girl I knew sat in the front seat. She smiled at me. We drove away. I was polite but, as he drove, I realised we were not heading for the party venue but to the other side of town where another party would take place the next day. We had arrived at the youth centre. He stopped the car and we all got out.

He was looking at me in a strange way and pulling out a large bunch of keys as he spoke.

'These are the keys the to front door entrance, then the internal doors. I knew you wouldn't be very pleased to cook the salmons now, with all the other things you've had to do. So I thought if I asked you for a date…'

I stared at him in disbelief.

'Well, anyway, here are the keys, and someone will pick you up in a couple of hours.'

I took the keys, hearing his words but not grasping their meaning. As he moved towards his car, his hand slipped for a second around the girl's shoulder. I could feel tears but was determined not to let my emotions show. She turned and threw me a triumphant glance. They drove away.

Damn it, he wasn't even special to me. He was my mother's choice. I let myself into the youth centre. I should have called a taxi and left then, but I had a conscience. I was still one of the organisers, with responsibilities, and obviously someone had not fulfilled their promises. The salmons needed to be cooked. The empty corridors slammed with the echo of heavy doors as I moved on into the steely kitchen where two large salmons lay wrapped in paper next to two purloined fish-kettles and a pile of vegetables to make a stock. I was totally alone. I washed and chopped the vegetables and slid the onions, carrots and celery into the vast fish kettles. I scaled the fish and some of the water spurted, staining my new dress. While lowering the fish on to the cooked vegetable beds I glanced at my nail-polished fingers – now chipped and smelly, and sobbed into the seasoned water.

By the time the fish lay cooling in their seasoned bath, to be lifted out of the water and skinned the next day, it was ten-thirty. I had been there almost two and a half hours. Someone should have come by now. Even with a time extension from my father because of the special escort, there would be very little party time left. I had scrubbed my hands as best I could but the stain on my dress stank and my eyes were swollen from crying.

Eventually, there was a clatter at the door. Someone had remembered me. I hid my face on the journey back to the party.

We walked into semi-darkness. The music was playing a rich slow smooch and some couples were enveloped in each other's arms in the centre of the room, whilst others were touching and petting on couches at the side. I felt even more alone. But, determined to make something out of the evening, I took a deep breath and decided to ask the visitors from away if they needed their glasses topped up. A slim dark-eyed man stood in the corner in the shadows and smiled hesitantly at me. I noticed his eyes crinkling with laughter. His dark hair was cropped very short.

'Can I get you a drink?' I asked.

'Looks like I'd better get you one,' he replied.

'I'd love one – Coke please.' I smiled.

He disappeared and returned with two glasses – his, a whisky and blackcurrant. We talked and found that we both lived in Cardiff, living parallel lives that were so close though we had never met. I even knew his best friend very well and saw him at my Sunday morning Hebrew class.

'Dance?' he said.

'But I stink of fish and vegetables,' I answered, embarrassed.

'At least you can cook,' he said.

We walked into the middle of the room to join the other couples. The Motown music pulsed with a thrumming beat. As we danced we talked and laughed, but during the few last tracks, started to move closer. We were staring at each other's faces and as I looked at his dark eyes edged with their thick lashes, I felt a starry explosion. The cynics would say that it was lust. But I knew that I was in love. My moment had come. We moved even closer together.

Then it became like a scene from Cinderella. I was looking at my watch and worrying about my parents' curfew. I explained my deadline. We left, dropping one of his friends home on the way. Finally, we parked under the darkness of the pine tree that shaded the glare of the street light and a romantic moon silvered the clouds. He slipped his arm around me and kissed me and I responded. I tasted the blackcurrant on his lips and felt his fingers slide through the layers of nylon. It seemed only seconds before it was time to go back into the house.

'Come out with me tomorrow?' he whispered.

'Yes, I will,' I answered, thinking that I would be able to go as that evening was already booked with my parents, because of the interfunction.

'I'll ring you, thanks for a lovely evening.'

I ran into the house. In the sitting room my mother sat in her oversized chair covered with sheets, banging at her stomach. She stared at me.

'You've been got at,' she scowled 'He did that? I'm surprised, I thought…'

'No, no, not him, I met someone else…he's asked me out for the party tomorrow.'

I didn't want to talk. I was still living the magic of his lips and hands. I could still hear his voice. Feel his gentle manner, his kindness.

'Mummy, can I get you ready for bed?'

'No,' she sulked, 'I'm not ready yet. Aren't you going to have your custard? You always have your custard after a party.'

'No thanks.' (I'd refused! My G-d, I'd refused!)

'So tell me what happened?'

'I met a lovely man. His name is Mervyn. He's an optician... twenty seven... and just opened a practice in James Howells and I think he's wonderful. But I'm stinking from cooking salmons and I'll have to have another bath... I'll make you a drink or something else if you want. Do you want something to eat, a bit of toast, a plain biscuit?' I started reciting the mantra of sick-food.

All the time, as I was speaking, I wanted to keep the sweetness of the evening perfect, cocooned in my mind. I knew I was in love. My first real love.

I left her downstairs and felt for the first time I had made my own decisions. I didn't eat as she wanted, and I hadn't been with the boy of her choice. There was a shift in our relationship that began at that moment. The fact that I'd said 'no' didn't excite or thrill me. Rather, it aggravated my guilt – I hated myself for not co-operating, for not agreeing with her, for not eating with her and maintaining that closeness that we had both enjoyed. But a new part of me had been awakened. I didn't want to eat. Food was not what I needed. I wanted to sing and laugh with joy and as I lay on my bed I kept remembering his soft mouth and the quiet manner and the whispered words and the eyes, his eyes, looking into mine.

Chapter Nine

Falling in Love

It was as if we had always been together. We both loved laughing and I remember the crazy times. On a glorious blue-skied day, we unpacked a picnic in a meadow studded with yellow buttercups and pink clover, while a lone cow stood at the end of a field swishing its tail. Suddenly, the cow turned towards us and began to move in our direction. We realised that we were not in a field with a cow. The animal was coming towards us at an increasing pace. We quaked all through the frantic, laughing, pack-up, finally escaping from the bull. Our best and most romantic dinners were when we sat in a pub, our corner lit with fairy lights, the music of Simon and Garfunkel soft in our ears, eating a simple fried egg on a bap and ice-cream drizzled with strawberry sauce.

I was dating once a week. He was working hard to build up a practice and I still wanted to complete my college work. So it didn't chafe to live within my father's restrictions. But as our love grew, it was natural to want more time together. A Saturday night, as well as the charity night on Wednesday evening, when he would call for me and take me home. Innocent dates, but not in my parents' eyes.

The opposition mounted. I was nineteen years old but I had to be back at home by eleven o'clock. My father tried his boyfriend-bullying tactics, but this new boyfriend was a man with his own business, who was not prepared to abandon his new-found girlfriend because of her father's tantrums.

Each time I returned from seeing him, the atmosphere was worse. They saw my growing love as a threat. We made dates and they would want me to cancel them. I spoke to them both.

'Mum, Dad, I love him and, one day, he's going to ask me to marry him – I just know it. Please, try to like him just a little.'

But they continued to attack. They said he was not the man for me. They mocked his hair-style, his teeth, his mode of dress, his time keeping.

'If he really loved you, he'd never be this late – you should find someone who is really keen to see you and makes proper time,' my mother would scowl disparagingly.

'But he's working and building up a practice, and if a new patient arrives late? And anyway, I don't mind…'

'No, you don't mind because you can't see these things…haven't you any pride? You're just throwing yourself at him.'

The rows escalated.

But circumstances had changed. I had tasted the gentle love of a man who wanted nothing more than to be with me and who enjoyed the sweetness of company without fighting. With that awareness came realisation that I was living in a crazy house. My family's shared routines of preparing and eating food had been lost, and both my father and myself were now refusing rather than taking food. The tenuous connection, that equation of love with food, had snapped forever, and they were blaming me for the rupture, although my father would often break his diet, go out and buy cakes or bake bread to challenge my resolve and then demand that I did the same. Very infrequently, especially if he had baked, I would eat some of his offerings, but his attempts to cook at home became rare and when he did try to sabotage my diet, my resolve was usually firm. My mother saw my diet as a personal affront. I was not her girl any more. I didn't love her. I didn't want to be with her. She concluded any argument with, 'You only want to be with him, not me.'

I was nineteen years old and in love and tired of the arguments. I'd look forward the whole week to my Saturday night. We'd talk on the phone nightly from Wednesday till Saturday, but when the weekend finally arrived, my inside would flutter with a thousand butterflies. I'd walk about the house singing the latest pop love song. By now I'd learnt the sound of his car engine and, as he sped into the road, I would call to my parents, 'He's here,' and run out and down the path to his car. It was easier to avoid my father's abusive taunts if I just left the house and Merv now rarely ventured inside. We learnt the rules of that game early. But I would have to be in by eleven and we'd spend the evening with eyes on our watches, tensely afraid of my father's fury.

Merv never understood the reason for their hostility. He was the same religion as me, very respectable, earning, and working, if anything, too hard.

The weeks passed. We knew that we were in love and that it was serious between us. We would now spend hours just talking, trying to discover a way to keep my parents happy and still allow us time together. My twentieth birthday approached. We'd both been offered hospitality by friends throughout the year and I wanted to return the favour by asking them to the house for coffee. I knew that a full party was out of the question. But I wanted to mark the occasion in some way. My parents acquiesced, especially when they knew that other eligible men would be invited. The plan was that I would borrow a few gentle-sounding records and, just for one evening, my mother would stay in her bedroom. I was very careful not to exceed the numbers allowed – they said a dozen in that large house would be fine. The morning of my birthday, my parents still seemed happy, kissed me – at least my mother did – gave me cards and wished me a happy birthday. During the day I made them both a special supper with decorated salads and stored it in the fridge so that they wouldn't suffer by eating upstairs for one night. For my friends, I made a chocolate cake and finger sandwiches, and I placed a few bowls of crisps and nuts about the room. As I removed the sheets and pillows from the large chair, I squirted air-freshener everywhere – just in case.

Just before the guests arrived my parents told me that there was a special box they would open with me after the party. Then they retired as planned upstairs with their meals, The Radio Times and the television. The bell rang. I knew it was Merv. We'd planned for him to come early so that we could share a few kisses before the others arrived. I ran to the door and we were in each other's arms and it was wonderful.

'Happy Birthday, love – it's just something little. I've never bought a present for a girl before. I don't know if…'

'I don't care…I'm thrilled…'

'It's a locket. I know you've always wanted one…I hope…'

I opened the small blue leather box. Inside was a tiny, dainty, locket on a gold chain. I was delighted. That tiny piece of gold symbolised so much.

'It's perfect…thank you.'

Our guests arrived. Merv helped me, taking the coats and pouring drinks – non alcoholic, of course, at my parents' request, but in the sixties there was less emphasis on alcohol. We played Peter Paul and Mary, Simon and Garfunkle, the Beatles and the Who. Later our friends sang 'Happy Birthday' and we dished out the cake. The evening was over. Merv helped me to hand out the coats and the group left.

My mother called down:

'Hasn't he gone yet? Isn't he gone yet? I need to get back to my chair now!' There was no 'need'. Her voice was angry. I'd done something wrong.

'I'd best go, love,' he said. 'I'll call you tomorrow.'

My guests had been half an hour later than scheduled. But that was not all. I knew that rebuking tone.

'Ruth, come up at once.' My father's voice and then my mother's:'I need you now!'

One last kiss and I shut the door and listened to Merv's footsteps walking away from the house.

'Up here at once, Miss,' called my father. 'How dare he, how dare he?'

I went upstairs.

'What? What did he do? He was so kind...he was so lovely.'

'Yes, we noticed how lovely he was, taking over our house, playing mine host. He thinks he owns the place already. He's waiting for us to die so that he can get his hands on the house. So what did the big lover, the great mine host give you?'

'He gave me a locket,' I sobbed.

'So let's see the grand present.'

I opened the box that would show them how much he loved me.

'That thing, that thing's – not worth tuppence!'

I took it out of the box. Sadly it was made for a child bridesmaid and was too small to reach around my neck. They laughed at each other.

'This is what we bought you.' My father threw an expensive jewellery box at my feet. I wanted to leave it there unopened.

'Well, go on...pick it up...open it.'

I opened the box to reveal a gold moonstone ring the stone in an oval setting surrounded by pearls.

'That is what we think of you. Never mind the rubbish he gives you.'

After that, the battles became worse. Every time I spoke to Merv, I was hounded. My parents managed to trash our time together. I became tired of fighting. I contemplated running away from home. But the old conditioning wouldn't release me. I was trapped by guilt and a terrible sense of duty. It was only a matter of time before I conceded defeat. We were, in those days, less independent. Only a small minority defied the authority of teacher, boss, or parent. Respect was the norm and duties were rigorously imposed.

Merv and I spent hours talking about my father and his cruelties and my mother's sad jealousy.

'I'm never going to be liked by them, whatever I do,' he said.

Finally, before a friend's Sunday lunch party, we drove to a local beauty spot, Castell Coch – a fairy-tale castle constructed by the Marchioness of Bute to entertain his friends. It is set on a hilltop, surrounded by a beech forest near Tongwylais, overlooking the main road to the valleys. There we talked over our problems.

'I love you,' he said. 'But I can't live like this any more… I can't be hated like this when I've done nothing wrong…it's not working – is it? Maybe, if we leave things for a while…maybe…they'll come round …Perhaps in a while…'

Castell Coch looked beautiful in the sunlight. The surrounding green of the forests was full with the soft booming sounds of wood pigeons and the chatter of rainbow-spotted starlings. Black ravens stalked the paths and scrounged titbits from the parked cars. As we left, the sunlight poured gold over the woodland below. But despite all the beauty of that spot, the sweet mossy-green smells, that day, the place felt as if it were inhabited by monsters.

At the party that followed, we stood at opposite ends of the room. Separated. Talking to others. I needed to go to his side and tell him that we mustn't let them spoil our lives, but I was bound by invisible chains. At the end of the party I discovered that my parents had arranged for another man – one of my parents' friends' sons – to escort me home.

'Such a nice boy,' they chorused.

'We've been friends with the parents for years…we know them…and he's…'

I did not argue. There was no point.

The weeks passed, and I pined for Mervyn. I'd lost hope. No one would ever replace the one I really loved. I was depressed and lonely. My parents gave me the odd dress, a trip away with other friends. In a state of suffocation I even agreed to become engaged to another man for a very short while, even though my feelings for him were entirely superficial. I liked him just as a friend. But I felt the situation was so hopeless: that if I couldn't have the man I loved then anyone would do, provided they were decent. After all, love had not brought me happiness. It seemed simpler to settle for second best – as long as that satisfied my parents.

Chapter Ten

It's my Party

4th May. My twenty-first birthday.

My father refused to have my friends in the house.

'The bloody hooligans can go in the garage. If you think I'm having that lot in...' he said. No point in arguing.

My mother made a plea on his behalf.

'After all, sweetheart, it's going to cost your father a lot of money to let you have this party. There's the cost of the food and the drink...'

So the garage it was. I decided to create a Hollywood-type Chinese opium den, although I was well aware that the reality bore no resemblance to my efforts. I borrowed old shiny and velour curtains from friends and hung them on the walls. For weeks I painted landscapes from encyclopaedias of Chinese scenes and copied Hokosai prints from the library on sheets of paper and mounted them. I created lamps by covering jam jars with red crepe paper and weighted them with sand. Then, on the night, I stuck cut candles inside and lit them, and the soft flickering lights hid the concrete corners of the room. The oil spot in the centre of the floor was covered by layers of newspaper and a worn-out rug. And the scent of garage was masked by strategically placed incense burners. I borrowed a few records and with a menu of sweet and sour meat-balls, oriental salads, with just-available bean sprouts and a revolutionary (for the time) dessert of tinned lychees mixed with mandarin oranges and pineapple, I hoped my friends would ignore the corner stack of old paint pots, lawn mower, and mound of tired deck-chairs. The preparations occupied my mind. But as busy as I was, I just wanted to be with Merv. Friends arrived, the walls throbbed to the sounds of 'Pretty Woman' and the Beatles and the party trembled into life. Merv was late. Eventually I saw him at the door. I wanted him to come over, hold me close, and tell me that we would be together again. But he was edgy, uncomfortable, particularly since my father, dressed in his old gardening trousers, a dirty shirt, and an even filthier expression, was leaning in the doorway. Merv left early. However, before he left, he told me that he planned to go away.

I had to see him. A few days later, I pretended I needed some information from the library, and instead I raced into Merv's practice. It was lucky he had no patients at the time. He took me into his consulting-room and told me that he was planning a trip to America. I looked into his eyes and my sense of loss had grown to a large dark lumpen ache. I needed to be with him but, after my party I was too nervous to say so. I needed to tell Merv and my parents that I loved him and needed him, whatever anyone thought. But I needed some sign from him, which didn't come.

A postcard arrived from Niagara.
  Went to the Montreal World Fair yesterday. Miss you
  Merv x
I walked about the house and college clutching that card, reading and re-reading the words 'Miss you', knowing that this was an echo of my feelings about him. Even though I would live with the guilt that I had not done enough for my mother, those two words finally told me that I had to change. I had to be with Merv. When I fell into bed after another bad evening with my mother, I lay twisting with worry, and when I finally slept, the same nightmare nagged my sleep. I was falling through space, through hollow buildings, some burnt, exposing scarred ribs, past empty eyeless windows then banging down flights of stairs, trying to clutch at something, anything to gain a finger-hold. Finally I landed

shaken and bruised in a blackened greasy basement. Above me, as in previous nightmares, swung a single light bulb, back and fore. I knew that I was totally alone.

It was as if my mother sensed his homecoming. Her depression deepened. There were rows about the way I served the food – I was too long with a hot drink, a cold drink, there was no butter knife, a flannel was – too wet or too dry, the thinnest slice of toast was too thin or too thick. Turn the television up, turn the television down. Another glass of lemon tea, you cut the lemon too thick…

'I need to go to the toilet now! You waited too long before carrying me back! You know how it hurts to sit there. You don't love me now I'm ill!'

In recent years, with the pain still raw, I have tried to understand the reasons why the sickness took such an irretrievable hold at that time. It was as if the anorexia became a kind of sucking parasite that not only consumed my mother's remaining flesh, but also took her inner self. She became another person. It sucked, twisted and violated her personality. Physically, the mother I loved was still present but her personality, 'The Sick Person', was no longer my mother. She had metamorphosed into another creature. I think it was then I started to mourn the loss of my mother. The change was so radical. I have read about other illnesses and find parallels in those suffering from Alzheimer's disease or in fact, any chronic disease that drags on over years. I wish I'd had the understanding at that time that I have now: the knowledge that comes with hindsight, after many years of mourning, questioning and wondering. I know now that my mother's reaction to my relationship with Merv was not the reaction of her true self; it was the reaction of the cruel, needy inner creature she had become.

My father…? My father just ran away, as he had always done. As he had done when my grandmother shook her fist at him, when the bombs fell in the war, whenever there was a crisis. Forced to be present, he began chameleon-like to assume my mother's characteristics. I had slipped through the looking glass and another place where Tweedledum and Tweedledee were in charge of my life. A few months on, I contracted a bad bout of shingles. The doctor was summoned. My mother resented his visit to me and told him that she was the one that needed him. He went to her, gave her time, wrote another piece of paper – the paper that bought the bottles and pills that fed and kept that damned ugly illness happy. Finally, he came to me in my small bedroom and sat wearily on the edge of my bed. He leaned over to me and stared into my face with his elderly yellowed eyes and whispered, 'Look, Ruth, a bit of advice. You have to get out of this house at all costs. I am warning you. This is not a safe place for you to be. If you remain you will become very sick. You must leave.'

I reminded myself of those words when I broke the house rules to restart my relationship with Merv. I felt that the sweet fine wire that joined us had strengthened in his absence. In my mind, our time apart had ended. As well as my other duties, I also had a duty to the man I loved.

I conceived a plan. On a Saturday morning while my mother recovered from another night of cramping pains and sickness, I rang Merv's receptionist. I could feel the thump of my heart in my chest, reverberating in my teeth, as I dialled the number. It sounded so loud I was afraid that somehow the noise would wake my mother.

'Hello, this is Ruth.'

'Hello, love. Sorry, I can hardly hear you. We haven't heard from you for a long time.'

'Yes, it's been difficult. But…I wonder, would you ask Mr Joseph when he comes in … you do expect him back today, don't you?'

'Yes, he's fully booked this afternoon.'

'Please could you ask him to ring me before he starts?'

'Of course, lovely to talk to you…Bye.'

The deed was done in a matter of seconds. As the receiver clicked I sat back on the red and cream Regency-striped chair in the hall and took a deep breath. What had I done? Suppose he didn't ring? Maybe I was wrong and he didn't feel the same way any more? Maybe he had met a girl in America who was not tied to such responsibilities as I was…? Would he want all the pain of our past again? I didn't know. I just had to carry on with my usual jobs, dead-heading house plants, chores in the kitchen, then to the loo to empty vomit bowl and bed-pans.

The morning dragged its feet as if it had blisters. All I could think about as I made a drink for my mother and ran her bath and helped her out with the usual panics, was that Merv might be unwilling to stand in the firing line again.

I needn't have worried. He started work at one pm and at twelve forty-five the phone rang.

'Hi, Ruth?' I could hear an unspoken jostle of questions like twittering birds. 'Did you ring? Did you want me? What did…?'

I cut in. My parents were both listening. My father was in his old beige gardening trousers with a cup of coffee in his hand. My mother was bathed, dried and had assumed her place on fresh pillows and sheets that I'd spread carefully on her chair. They both looked at me, unbelieving. I knew I must say nothing about having rung his office earlier. This phone call must appear to have come from him. Otherwise they would know that I had broken the rules, deceived them.

'Oh, yes, I'd love to go for coffee.' He could refuse.

'A coffee? Oh yes! Yes, fine, yes, yes! OK! I'll pick you up at eight, OK?

The moment I heard his voice I knew I had made the right decision. He sounded so happy. It was only later I realised how risky the plan had been. He could have been going somewhere, especially since I heard that night that he had been elected the President of the South Wales Opticians and there would be functions to attend: balls and dinners. He was now a busy man, with a successful practice.

The sound of his car engine to me that night was like a fanfare of trumpets. I ran out, down the path and into his arms. He drove me away from the house, from the fears and anguish of that place. For a few sweet delicious hours, I was out of prison with the man I loved, who loved me. The memory of that evening is so dipped in sweetness that it is sugared to a blur. But I do remember him asking me:

'Does this mean that we are together and that you are going to be my girlfriend?'

'Yes, please. If you'll have me.'

When I returned home, I expected a row. But the house was unexpectedly silent. My parents must have talked. That night as I lay in my bed with the memory of his arms holding me, I felt like a princess who had been locked away in a tower with an ogre – the ogre being the illness, not my mother – now rescued by my knight in shining armour.

Chapter Eleven

New Battles Old Wars

The next day both my parents asked me if I'd had a pleasant evening. They asked so innocently I misconstrued their behaviour as accepting Merv at last. But now I know that they were simply baffled and were retreating for a while until they had time to formulate a plan of campaign. Though I am sure they were genuinely pleased to hear me singing again. But, soon, the old arguments were slipping into my earshot –

'He's too old for you – he's not religious enough, he's too religious…If he's so keen on you why doesn't he ask you to marry him? He just wants to mess you about.' Anything that they could throw at me that might change my mind.

But Merv and I had an understanding. We were just happy to be together. He was establishing a new practice and finances were difficult. And our lives, woven together, were creating the stuff of memories. We'd spend evenings in the country watching rabbits night-hopping, sniffing the starry air, their white scuts bouncing in reflected light. Sometimes we'd drive out to the coast and stare at the dark sea, twisting and rolling, breaking into strings of frothy beads on the rocks. Or we'd marvel at the creaking heaviness of a flight of air-borne swans arrowing over our local lake. He showed me the sweet chestnut tree in his school's park and we tried to pick wimberries at the top of his special mountain, but ended up laughing and kissing so much that we took home only four berries in our Tupperware tub, to his mother's veiled amusement.

He took me to his hometown Merthyr for the afternoon and gave me a tour of his old haunts.

'This is where I used to get my sweets and this is where my mother got her meat' – an interesting butcher's shop with one half of the shop dedicated to Jewish customers and the other for Gentiles. Legend describes how the system worked well for years, until one day nearly all the Jewish community received liver in the same week. Mervyn's mother and her friends were so delighted that it was their turn, and not a special occasion, that they commented when they saw each other. But the community was only killing and using the front quarters of one animal per week. One liver between a whole community? The butcher was supplying the Jewish community with livers from animals that had not been killed by the rabbi.

'And this is where we lived and we used to go to school there, yes, it's a castle built by the ironmasters, the Crawshays, to entertain their friends, now a museum. And we had to walk up that path to the synagogue, high on the hill, fine in the summer but in the winter with ice on the road it was treacherous.'

His life was imbued with love for the history of the place. He took me to see viaducts, and canals and other castles. I loved him even more for his passion and his knowledge. Finally, a year after that invitation for coffee, we drove one evening to one of our favourite places. The backdrop was a group of oil-storage containers. Sounds so unromantic, but their dark magnitude was illuminated by thousands of tiny white lights and in the foreground, on a piece of barren land, we watched the hop and jump of rabbits bouncing in the summer air.

'OK, then,' he said. 'Will you marry me?'

'What, no on the knees stuff? Just OK, then? Do you realise I will remember this for the rest of my life?' But of course I agreed. Neither of us told anyone anything that night. I managed to get away the next night, which was a huge privilege for me and we celebrated with a trip to the fun-fair where we popped our heads into the photo booth and took our 'engagement photos' and he threw quoits in a stall and won a fluffy orange banana with stuck-on eyes. My engagement present. I went home. This time my mother was still up sitting in her chair. Was it my imagination? Had she lost even more weight? How could I tell her that I wanted to leave home? Merv and I had discussed our plans together for hours. But first I had to tell her.

'Mummy, Merv has asked me to marry him and I've said yes. I hope you're pleased. You know I've only ever loved him. Please say you're happy...'

I watched her face – each miniscule bone on cheek and jaw working painfully together like an anatomy lesson. She tried to make an effort.

'Yes, yes, love, I am pleased for you. I'm very pleased.'

And I know, at that time, she genuinely felt that way.

'He wants to come and speak to Daddy and ask for my hand – when can he come?'

She changed her position and I watched the agony reflected on her face.

'As soon as Daddy comes in, I'll tell him and ask him. I won't phone.'

I realise now that the news had to be broken gently: that despite my mother's efforts to be pleased, my father would be unhappy, unable to cope with the practicalities of a new life alone with my mother. Eventually he returned and I had to make him coffee and leave them alone – as if she had to break bad news to him. She was already excited at the prospect of being the mother-of-the-bride and organising a very large party. But I had to leave the room and I suspect my father's reaction was not so joyful.

It was agreed that my father would see Merv the next day and I watched my father put a bottle of champagne in the fridge and my mother instructed me to take out some of the best glasses. Too good to be true, I thought, anxiously. When Merv arrived, it was like a scene from a bad sit-com. Merv had to chase my father around the garden. Dad wouldn't stay still. Finally Merv cornered him in a section of the herbaceous border. Even then my father would not answer. He was still running away. Merv had to almost shout at him that he wished to marry me. However, my father then gave his permission and his blessing, and we enjoyed a very wonderful and rare moment where we were all happy and sharing and looking forward to the future. My parents agreed to remain silent until I had met Merv's parents and then we would be properly engaged.

Meeting Merv's parents was a scary prospect. I had very little experience of other families apart from calling for the occasional friend from school and this was an occasion of such magnitude. But I needn't have worried. Gertie and Nathan were late preparing the celebration tea and we drove around the local countryside a few times until all was ready. I remember that Gertie wore a powder-blue linen dress trimmed with wooden beads. She was a very quiet lady, small in stature, but she held her head with great gentility and Nathan wore the largest beaming smile. The table was laid with fine bone china as if for dignitaries, and it was then I discovered that Gertie made the best lemon drizzle cake I've ever tasted. But sweeter than all of the cakes on that table was the welcome.

'If you are going to be my daughter-in-law, then I will treat you exactly as my daughter,' said Nathan, giving me a rather sloppy kiss. He remained true to his word. I couldn't believe that it was possible to spend so much time with people without fighting or bad moods. I began from the first day to slot into that household as if I had always lived with them. There would never be as special a place as the chair in front of the blazing fire, sitting opposite my mother-in-law, laughing over discussions of people and events, enjoying her phenomenally dry humour, always with a slice of home-made cake and a cup of rich mahogany tea.

But as the Josephs made me more welcome, the situation in my own home deteriorated. My father was beginning to realise that I was going to move out of the house and despite my promises to live close and come every day from lunch-time till supper time to look after my mother, the prospect of losing his freedom at the other times must have terrified him. His anger and moods were frequent, attacking Merv's status and looks. He insisted on an eleven month engagement even though we wanted to marry relatively quickly. He was routinely difficult about dates. Merv bought tickets for us to see Freddie and the Dreamers at Porthcawl. We were so excited until we realised that the stars would only be performing in the second half of the show, and it would not start until after nine. I had to be back at eleven and the venue was an hour's drive away.

'Oh, he'll understand for once. He wouldn't want to spoil our treat,' Merv said.

We found a phone box and rang to ask if was it alright to be late just once. But my father became angry and said, 'You should never take her so far away from Cardiff. No, it is not alright. Bring her home now!'

Merv also bought tickets for a staff evening at a night-club just out of Cardiff, but was berated by my father for considering that he could possibly take me to such a den of iniquity. (My father had never been there.) So Merv had wasted yet more money on tickets. My father became a sterner clock-watcher. Often he would be standing in his shirt-sleeves at the doorway as I returned home so that we had to forgo our good-night kiss. As I walked back into the house, I would feel the walls closing in like a prison.

Eventually, the date of the wedding was set for 1st July, Investiture Day. In theory a good idea as it was to be an extra national holiday. My mother and I started planning colours and flowers and dresses.

We threw an engagement party in October, and two hundred people were invited for an 'at home' between three and five. Everyone arrived at four o'clock and the house became jammed with guests. The waitresses locked themselves into the larder with the smoked salmon sandwiches and the sparkling wine, and I was afraid of anyone touching me as I had spent the last month recovering from shingles. Old friends who had been special in my mother's life years before were forced to push their way through the house in a conveyer belt of humanity and arrived at the other end squashed and gasping for air. It was a farce. After that disaster, my mother became desperately sick on several occasions, each time needing my care to rescue her from the clutches of hospital and drips. Often my evenings with Merv were curtailed. I worried whether he would have the patience to want to stay with me.

Just after the Passover, and three months to the date of our wedding, my parents arranged with Merv's parents to meet for tea at Bindles, which was a theatre, ballroom and tea-room at the sea-side town of Barry, twelve miles up the coast from Cardiff, to finalise wedding details. Bindles was the proposed reception venue. We were invited to listen to the discussions. My father took Merv and I in the back of his car without warning us that he had taken the seats out of the back, ready for the stock to be loaded that night, so we rolled around on the floor for the half-hour journey feeling bruised and sick. However, after 'the chat', which seemed to go well, we were allowed to leave the party and spent some time on our own sitting on the pebbles contemplating our wedding day and enjoying the sun. On the journey back my mother hardly spoke to me, which I did think surprising considering her earlier excitement. But I just assumed that she was tired and needed a rest. However, the next day, my parents called me into the lounge. My father looked grave and there was a twisted expression on his face which I had never seen before.

'Ruth, you're going to be very upset when we tell you this, but you have to know the facts. When we talked to Gertie and Nay yesterday, they said that they were very much against your marriage because Merv is desperately ill and the whole wedding thing could kill him.'

I sat down. I could feel green-nausea crawling over my body.

'But he's fine, he's fine…I know he's…'

'Please don't argue. We are telling you this for your own good. Gertie and Nay told us that when he comes in from work, he is so exhausted that he passes out and he only manages after a long while to drag himself together and summon up enough energy to take you out. Even *he* doesn't know the extent of his illness. But suffice to say, if you marry him – the shock could kill him.'

'How ill is he…?'

'That we don't know, but certainly he'll have a longer life if you don't marry him. And you mustn't discuss this with him either because he doesn't realise how very ill he is.'

I ran upstairs to my room and fell on the bed sobbing. The man I loved was sick, so sick I must not even speak to him about it. All our plans, all our hopes dashed. I hardly spoke that day, just walked around in a daze making my parents' food, washing up and helping my mother with the toilet and her washing. All I could hear was their words banging back and fore in my mind like some crazy ball-game.

Desperately ill, desperately ill.

Merv was late that evening – it was after eight when I heard his car and I ran out to met him.

'Hey, love, what's the sad face for? Is your mum?'

'No…no, nothing like that.'

'Well, what? Have they made another rule, have we got to be in even earlier?'

'No, no, I can't say. I'm not allowed to say.'

'I'm going to get you a cup of coffee. You look terrible…When you've had it you can tell me what's wrong. Come on, it's the end of April. Only three months to go and we'll be married.'

My mind was shrieking. Should I say anything to him? I could kill him. I sobbed for most of that evening. Until eventually the words fell out.

'I don't care – I'd rather have a couple of months with you married…if you're that ill, than no time together at all.'

'What's that? What do you mean I'm ill? How am I ill?'

'Your parents told my parents that you were desperately ill and the shock of us marrying could kill you. And I wasn't supposed to say…because that could also kill you. And I so love you…and… I…'

'Wait, love, wait. How can I be ill? Do I look ill?'

'You pass out – lose consciousness before you see me and you just about manage to get yourself together to take me out. You're hiding some terrible illness from me. And from yourself.'

'But, love, think. How is that possible? I work until seven most evenings… later other nights. Then I dash home in the car, wash and shave and have something to eat and I'm picking you up by eight. When is there the time for me to collapse?'

'I don't know, but my parents told me…it must be the truth… and…'

He kissed me. Kissed my eyes. My tears now ran with relief and joy, but also with appalled distress at my parents' lying.

Over thirty five years later, I look back on this event and realise the stupidity of my trusting nature. My only defence is that I had always believed what my parents told me. They had not, to my knowledge, lied before. But the thought of losing their nurse must have been terrible for them to contemplate. My mother, understandably, was petrified to be alone, whilst my father could see his future trapped within the confines of the house.

But from then on I also understood our doctor's warnings. That desperate lie firmed my resolve. I would marry my fiancée though I would still try to look after my mother as much as my marriage would allow.

Our wedding plans continued. What with the catering plans, Jewish *kashrut* problems, and the worries about clothes to fit my mother, Merv and I contemplated eloping or getting me pregnant to scupper the event. I was still living by my father's strict laws. In by eleven o'clock although now allowed to see each other twice a week. My father was still going away on business and I would stay with my mother all day and all night, now I had passed my exams, ensuring that my few hours with Merv would not cause her problems. When it was time to go out, I'd fill a thermos with soup made during the day in case she felt like a taste – 'Don't forget I like it very thin and very tasty and make sure there are no fat eyes on the top at all' – and fill another flask with of hot water. Next to that on a tiny bone-china dish I'd place some lemon slices and some tea-bags and a small tin of Marie biscuits, or thin arrowroot and a few poached peaches. Her eating went in phases rather like clothes fashions. Occasionally she'd fancy grated salads. They took an age to make and much energy. I'd grate carrots and apples and cucumber and pickled dill cucumbers with a plastic grater and combine the mixture. It was quite a sharp concoction and she'd always suffer afterwards. But I could understand her fancy for something not so bland.

I tried, dammit. I tried to make her as comfortable as I could. Once I forgot to put out a small knife and she was angry, and once, leaving the house in daylight, I forgot to put on the large light above her and she said that I'd

151

neglected her. I strove hard to show her that I cared but she always complained that she no longer had my love.

'I can love you as well, Mummy, I do really love you…Honestly.'

'No, you don't. Now that you've got him you don't think of me any more…you don't want me now. I'm a nuisance. I just get in the way.'

Stupid – all these years later and the hurt still stabs like it's new.

I was, at that time, like two people: one that lived in the house and tried to placate the furies, plumped up the pillows, emptied the bed-pans, bathed the bedsores and smoothed flesh with cream, and, as the clock struck eight, the other: a girlfriend who wore just a dab of lipstick, a smear of eye-shadow and a hint of mascara, and was still often wearing the dark-green lisle tights that had lasted interminably from sixth form days and would not wear out. We never threw away if there was still some use. My parents' war-time training. But Merv just laughed at them, kissed me and called me 'cabbage stalks'.

Around this time Merv brought round to our house an old friend called Norman, a very amiable chap who was visiting from London. Mervyn, Norman and I were all going out for supper together. Merv introduced him to my parents and was told to sit down and relax. Norman watched as I ran about the house in a pinny, finishing jobs and settling my mother for the evening. Even though I was having dinner out with Merv and Norman, my father still insisted that I prepared his meal and washed up, and put every dish away before I was allowed to leave. Eventually, I removed my apron and ran laughing out of the kitchen.

'This is Ruth,' Mervyn said.

Later, Norman confided to Merv that he thought I was the maid.

152

Each time, as I shut the front door and ran down the path I had to struggle to discard my caring life. I had to forget about measuring pills out and noxious-smelling fluids, the fact that my legs ached from all the journeys up and down the stairs, or the dull throbbing of my tired back that had carried a five stone load of bones back and fore to a toilet. Forget about the smell of vomit and worse. Very few people saw the inside of our house, and those that did enter saw little of the truth. They came for tea, sandwiches, cakes, stayed a while and left. But they never witnessed the dark reality. For the few hours they were there, my mother would make a massive effort to entertain, be charming, be her old self. Flying on the temporary buzz of adrenaline, she was still the best entertainer. She would organise the food – we'd cut the crusts off like in the olden days, lay the best china, make the most tempting array, get out the smoked salmon and slice the cake. She would be the queen. But after the visitors left she would be exhausted, gasping for breath, bereft because the tea-party was over. It was as if the occasion was able to drag her off her own nasty carousel of suffering for a short while, but the energy required left her even more sick. Sometimes, too, the tea parties would upset her. She was more sensitive than anyone I've ever known and if someone said something out of turn there would follow hours and hours of: 'What did they mean? Why did they say that? Did they think…? More hurt and suffering, and everything out of proportion in her topsy-turvy, unbalanced world. She still rang my grandmother, out of duty, every day despite the fact that they hated each other, and this aggravated her distress. She waved goodbye to my father deeply resenting his absence – and his behaviour when he was away would upset her. He would phone from Bristol from one of the best hotels and complain that there was rat poison placed in doorways and that he was suffering, and my mother would believe it. He would ring her supposedly from his room and tell her that the source of music and laughter she could hear was from the television. He would tell her that he lived on bread rolls and snacks in his room, but later when I met some members of that other life they told me how he was well acquainted with the head waiter in the hotels he visited and what fun socially he was. He was a bad liar and the lies became larger. Easy to suspect – easy to detect. Frightening in their effect on my mother.

Yet, there was a generous side to his character. He was renowned for being an over-generous tipper. When we were out as a family (which was extremely rare, but now and then my mother was able to manage the journey to have a cup of tea in the local store, which would cost six old pennies) my father would tip ten shillings. Most of the staff would be delighted, hoping that they would be the ones to gain his favour but I suspect he was an object of derision to the more discerning staff. He would spend wild amounts on bouquets of flowers for my mother – flashy gestures to smooth out the wrinkles of suspicions my mother might have. Each time he went away, he returned with a piece of jewellery. My mother left them to me but I have given them all away, despite the fact my mother treasured them. For me, they became symbols of disrespect and betrayal. I cannot sustain any myth about Geoffrey as a truthful, caring, husband and father. The Jewish religion is very specific in its laws that one should honour thy father and thy mother, but when I have attempted to follow these laws I have suffered from guilt. It is not honest. Of course I appreciate that my father was living with a sick woman for most of his life and that was a tragedy for him. But I am now a mother and grandmother, whose first instinct is to protect her children, and I cannot understand how he as a father could dump his obligations on to his child, if he loved her. And the fact that he did, hurts.

But during our engagement there were also good times. There were dances and new friends and sipping Coke or coffee in coffee bars. We would take evening walks by the

sea at Cold Nap where we'd hold hands and listen to the
rush of the waves. Sometimes we'd drive down the country
lanes at the back of my parents' house. We discovered a
tumbledown ruin which we christened 'our house' where we
felt safe and laughed at silly jokes and exchanged our kisses.
On a picnic during the Passover he picked me a few
mountain primroses and I saved and pressed them. We
walked through damp forests relishing the deep violet scent
of bluebells, just waiting, counting the days, when we would
be a couple.

My life with Merv was becoming richer and more
exciting with each meeting. He told me stories of his early
life in the Welsh Valleys. How when he was seven his
mother gave him a live turkey to be killed at the kosher
slaughter house, warning him not to untie the top: it was
bagged in a flexible shopping basket with the handles tied
together. And how when he saw his best friend in the High
Street, he found showing off irresistible.

'What you got there?' said his friend.

'A live turkey!' boasted Merv.

'Let's see.'

'Not allowed to open...'

'Oh, go on...bet there's not one there...'

'Alright then, here...'

He untied the handles of the basket and the turkey,
seeing his chance of freedom, burst from the basket,
tumbling the boys and raced up Merthyr High Street with
two young lads in pursuit. Most of the High Street became
part of the chase.

He had sneaked into the ends of football games,
scrumped apples and been a lad and I loved him for his
mini-misdemeanours. And loved the way his parents forgave
him and now laughed at his pranks.

The date of the marriage grew closer. It was time to find
somewhere to live. Merv had only been self-employed for a
short while and, with being in college and caring for my

mother, I had no income of my own. We had to find somewhere within a restricted budget. My father discovered an elegant four-bedroomed cottage which he said we should purchase. The cottage backed on to my parents' house.

'It's perfect,' my father said. 'We'll knock down the fence between the two houses and you'll be able to look after your mother as before…'

'And your father can still go away on business,' chimed my mother innocently.

We could never have afforded the house anyway. It was totally out of our price-range. But even if we had been able to, we both felt it was vital that we started out with a good distance between parents and children. I could still hear the doctor's warnings echoing in my ears. The consequent rows made me feel like a traitor. Eventually we found a semi-detached house nine tenths of a mile from both parents' houses (we tested the distance on the car's milometer). But my mother's resentment still boiled daily.

'You only think of him now. The minute that ring's on your finger, you'll forget we exist. You won't want to know me any more. I'll just be your old mother.'

'I promise you, Mummy, I won't.'

And I kept promising her. But as the wedding got nearer, each crisis seemed to spell more calls in the night to our patient, rheumy-eyed doctor. I was scared. There was only so much my poor mother's body could take. The picture of her illness was darkening. The vomiting and diarrhoea was now so automatic that every night was 'a bad one'. And this would be followed by cramps in her legs and stomach and she would scream with the pain. Every night I prayed that things would improve. But they didn't. Although in the daytime, as if some farce writer wrote the pages of our lives, we would return to the semblance of a loving family preparing for a wedding.

I managed to steal a few hours away on my own and saw a wedding dress that I loved. It was a pretty dress fashioned out of cheapish lace but effective and only eighteen pounds – more than enough for the day. It was a fashionable style, high-necked, leg of mutton sleeves edged with small frills and a fitted waist, and I loved it. I felt 'with it'. I told my parents, describing the dress, thinking they'd be pleased that I was planning such an economical choice.

My mother sat in her big chair in the lounge covering her mouth with apprehension as my father bawled at me, scorning my taste, almost lunging at me, wanting to hit but just controlling his fists and the boiling fury that seemed to pour through his whole body. 'Do you want people to laugh at me?'

'Why laugh?'

'That I can't buy you a decent dress.'

'But it's pretty. I like it.'

'Yes, of course, it's all about you, isn't it? It only matters that you like it. You don't realise that all the gown manufacturers are coming to the wedding and they will laugh at a cheap dress. How can you think of it? Rubbish, rubbish lace.'

'But a gown is such a waste of money and a huge wedding is a…'

'You'd like that if people said we couldn't give you a decent do.'

'No, I just wish that things could be smaller.'

'No arguments. You'll go to London with your mother and she'll pick out something decent.'

So we went to London – a difficult trip, trying to ignore the stares that followed my mother's tiny body wherever she ventured out. She was now so frail that people would openly gaze and comment, even point to her wasted stick legs and arms or the black shadows under her eyes. They had seen a walking cadaver, been on the ghost train. I even heard one person commenting loudly that it was wrong to allow ordinary people to see such a sight. I pretended I hadn't heard and propelled my mother in a different direction. But at the same time I realised how my ordinary day was peppered with revulsion and how habit and the repeat of the grim had inured me to it. I no longer saw what others could see. I was accustomed to horror because it was my life.

But we did manage the train journey to London and a taxi to the hotel. Then we had to put up with the performance of room service and my mother's disgusted impatience with their offerings. Another difficult night was made worse by the standardisation of a British menu – 'sorry we don't make toast after four, only meat sandwiches or cheese sandwiches, chicken and chips now or tomato soup,' and other lack of facilities, and then the next day we had breakfast in the room – something I've hated ever since. Another prison with a different décor, hemmed in with food and the smells and sounds of evacuation in a locked and curtained room not able to see the outside world or its inhabitants. Then, in the late morning, we took a taxi to the chosen bridal house. My mother plucked a little energy from the air assisted by the thought of buying an outfit.

I saw revolted looks from the ladies behind the counter as we entered the shop but they were quick to mask their faces. Mum scanned the rows of dresses: glorious chiffons, sleek sculptured dresses figured with lace and beads, cutesie sixties baby-doll dresses.

'Ah – that's the one,' she said. 'Try that.'

'But Mummy, it's heavy satin and I'm getting married in July!'

'It's suitable. It's got long sleeves and a high neck so it will please the religious members of the family. You know you must not show anything…'

'But Mummy, don't you think that shiny satin is just a little bit fattening?'

'It's fine.'

I put it on. My mother deemed it appropriate. I thought it was heavy and certainly not as pretty as the little lace I'd seen in the store in Cardiff. But there was no point in saying anything. It was Mummy's do, after all. She chose my dress. But I picked out a small headdress embellished with plastic pearls, and a veil. Then we turned our attention to her clothes. The only outfit that even remotely fitted her was a lime green dress and coat in an acetate fabric, in a tiny size six. Even so when she tried it on, reams of cloth hung spare about her small body. The style was classic but the designer had stuck nasty plastic flowers around the hem of the dress and the collar. The sales girl assured us that they could be left off – we would receive two new outfits that were replicas of those we had tried on, made specially in our size. My mother was happy. Buying shoes for her was difficult but when large insoles were glued into place in a pair of tiny navy shoes, she was able to visualise herself on the day.

By this stage in our wedding preparations I was so looking forward to my new life as wife, that the ceremony itself seemed almost incidental – a monumental fuss. But my mother's enthusiasm increased daily. Here was her opportunity to shine once more. Unfortunately her standards of perfection defied anyone else's comprehension. The guest list grew as she remembered old friends and family.

I broached the subject of guests after I'd cleared up supper one evening and served the coffee and cake. I'd brought in my father's slippers and set the paper next to the fruit.

'Daddy. Do you think I could ask some of my friends to the wedding?'

It was as if I'd lit the paper of a fast-burning firework. He threw down the paper and blew.

'Have you any idea what this whole bloody thing is costing!'

Mum blurted, 'Don't call it a bloody thing, Geoff. I've tried really hard to make it special.' Then there were tears from her and an extra banging of her stomach in time to the pain of the argument.

'I know that, but she thinks I'm made of money, that it just grows on bloody trees.'

'No, I don't, Daddy. It's just that Merv and I have already been invited to two weddings and…'

'You may have three couples. Finished. I want no more discussion on this.'

I did not argue. I had accepted that my wedding day would be my mother's day, a substitute, perhaps, for her disastrous marriage. It was also her swansong. The swansong of the beautiful entertainer, the one who did everything perfectly. Her plans escalated further and my father dabbed his face with an immaculate handkerchief as the lists extended to mammoth proportions: two hundred and fifty people for a sit-down salmon lunch, the same for a chicken dinner in the evening, some invited for both with a strawberries, meringues and champagne tea to fill in the gap. (People brought outfits to change for dinner).

The presents began to arrive. At the end of the sixties present lists were unusual and considered a little vulgar. So boxes of items arrived wrapped in the taste and generosity of the giver. We did not smoke but we were given cigarette lighters, ashtrays, and cigarette boxes in onyx. Seven soda water siphons arrived (we drank rarely) and five stainless-steel carving platters (we hardly ate meat). People gave us plates they had bought with Green Shield stamp coupons and sets of Pyrex dishes to my mother's taste. We didn't care. Being together was all that mattered. However, the presents caused my mother great agitation. She needed to be the one who did the unwrapping, and exclaim at the good/ bad/ indifferent taste. If the present was generous my mother could not cope, and often wanted it. In the end, we came to an arrangement: I left the presents for her to open and if there was anything that she fancied, it was hers to take. She made herself comfortable with this by saying, 'After all it is your father who is really paying for all of this. It's right that I get the pick.'

160

'Take Mum, take.' I just wanted to be with my future husband.

With ten days to go to our wedding, our clothes arrived. My dress, purporting to be an exact replica of the sample in the shop, was a size larger. I had also lost weight so the whole garment stood about me like a stiff, shiny, extra body. And the arms had been sewn in back to front. So, off the hanger, they curled towards my back. My mother's dress and coat were the garments she had tried on in the shop. They had just pulled the plastic flowers off and clumps of glue sat taunting her in their place. My poor darling mother with her history as fashionista was expected to wear an outfit embellished with glue marks. After hours of her hysterical sobbing, we rang contacts and eventually found a lady who unpicked, cut and re-sewed my dress, replacing the sleeves in the right position, then cutting out hefts of material to make the whole thing smaller. The glue lumps were hastily scraped off and covered with bugle beads, but my mother hated the whole outfit and was no longer looking forward to wearing it. It seemed like a bad omen.

During these last few weeks, rows occurred with increased frequency. I did not wake my mother at precisely the right moment. The tea was too strong, it was too weak. Merv was phoning me and I was wasting time when there were other things to do. I was late running the bath, too early running the bath. And my father still insisted on an eleven o'clock curfew.

Neither Merv nor I planned a stag or hen night, but at the last minute my mother decided to hold an eve-of-wedding party for her closest family and friends. Neither Merv nor his family were invited. That evening, the night before the wedding, I had planned a slow bath painting my nails and setting my hair. Instead I was chasing around the kitchen preparing and laying a meal for twenty; any other time I would have been delighted to give my mother the pleasure of entertaining, but not that evening. And I was hurt. I had wanted Merv's parents to be invited. But my request was ignored. Merv brushed it off.

'Don't worry, love. My mother's very quiet anyway. I think she'd prefer a rest the night before a big do, anyway.'

But secretly I suspect he was upset.

In the early hours of the morning, I fell into bed exhausted. Then lay wide awake, thinking of the huge changes about to occur in my life. Wondering, worrying and hoping.

Chapter 12

Mr Tambourine Man

A new chapter but the same music. I'd listened child-like to the tales of marriage. That a bride's day is the happiest day of her life and that she is going to be happy ever after. Happy, happy, happy – but not in our house.

It was my wedding day. I'd set my alarm but lay watching the illuminated hands of my Westclox drag their way around the face for hours. I went downstairs. My father's face scowled at me.

'You OK, Dad? Exciting, isn't it?'

'What's so bloody exciting? It may be for you. There's nothing exciting for me.'

I made him coffee, but he stormed past me and out of the kitchen. It's an emotional day, a wedding day. But I honestly thought that that day my father would pretend to be happy for me. Watching the clock until exactly the right minute, I made a tray of tea with a fresh rose cut from the garden in a vase and on an embroidered tray cloth put a single sliver of melba toast on a bone-china plate next to the cup of lemon tea. I pushed open the door to my mother's room.

'Mummy, are you OK?'

'No.'

'What's the matter?'

'I'm not coming. I'm too ill. You don't need me, anyway.'

'But Mummy, of course I do.'

'Well, I'm not coming!'

I took a deep breath and tried to be positive hauling out the bright nursery attitude that I sometimes needed, to pull her away from the brink.

'Oh Mummy, you often feel really bad when you wake up. Have a drink and you'll feel better. The hairdresser's going to be here soon.'

'I don't care. I'm not getting up. There's no point.'

I could feel the tears pushing into the back of my eyes. But I didn't want red eyes and a red nose for my wedding day.

'Please Mummy…please, will you get up…it's my wedding day.'

'You don't care about me…you don't want me…you only want him. I said he'd take you away from me!'

'That's not true. I really love you and I really love him. I can love him and you and…and anyway, what will people think? All those guests waiting for you.'

The doorbell rang; I think it was the flower delivery – a button-hole for my father, a corsage of freesias for my mother and a small fragrant bouquet of freesias, roses, sweet-peas and lily of the valley for me. Miraculously, the sound of the outside world, coupled with my last words, stirred my mother. She had a duty to her public. I ran a bath for her. She moved stiffly, lowering herself painfully into the water, and I brought soft towels to dry her and lifted her out. Then the hairdresser arrived and my hair was dampened down and set and I was placed under a mobile hair-dryer. A few quiet minutes of contemplation for a bride. A time to revel in the excitement of the moment. Instead, I shook with new anxieties and misgivings.

It was the hairdresser who helped me into my dress just as the photographer came to the door. My moment had come. The satin dress had been altered and fitted silkily close to my body. My mother fixed my veil and kissed me.

'Please, darling, don't let him take you away from us. Don't let him…'

'Mummy, he won't. He loves me and he really wants to be part of our family…'

'Ruth!' my father screamed from downstairs. 'Aren't you ready yet? The photographer's here and you need to get a move-on.'

I walked downstairs to stand, as directed, in my father's rose garden.

'Hey, Daddy, what do you think?'

'Bloody waste, for him.'

'Please, Daddy, please.'

The photographer tried to ignore the blackness that hung about my father as he stormed back and fore.

'Move over there, please, to that bank of roses – yes, the pink ones. That should make a wonderful picture. Now, smile,' he said encouragingly. He darted about, trying to smooth the troubled atmosphere. My father scowled at the camera.

'Take her hand…look at your daughter…it's her day,' the photographer pleaded.

'My day, Daddy,' I begged, looking into the furrows of his face.

'Look, Ruth, I've said it before and I'll say it again, it's not too late to cancel the whole bloody shower. Just say the word. It's still not too late.'

'But I want to marry him. I love him.'

'Then there's nothing more to say.'

'Won't you give me your blessing?'

'No.'

No kiss – never a kiss. In fact I don't think I can ever remember my father hugging or kissing me.

The cars arrived and I returned to help my mother with her final preparations. The hairdresser who set her golden hair chatted with a light busy voice, excited at being part of a wedding. She persuaded my mother to get dressed at last.

Mum stood in her lime green dress, desperately emaciated, her tiny legs and arms looking like narrow, fleshless sticks.

'Mummy, you look lovely.'

'I hate my dress and I hate my shoes – nothing goes.'

'It looks good and it fits you really well.'

I helped my mother down the stairs and a car arrived containing my grandmother who looked equally as miserable. An older version of her son. And then our car arrived – a claret-red Rolls Royce, a present from the store where my future husband had his optical practice. My father looked out of the window.

'Trust him to get a bloody red one. Anyone would think it's a celebration.'

I climbed into the cavernous leathery interior with my father, leaving my poor mother to travel with my grandmother. These days in Jewish weddings the mother travels with the bride, as the father goes early for prayers. But not in my day. I wished that I could have made that special journey with my mother and tried to reassure her, tried to soothe some of the feelings of loss she was experiencing. As it is, I can remember nothing of that journey with my father. How did my mother cope with my grandmother? I don't know. Did my mother cope with her nausea in the car with my grandmother watching her? How did she get to the synagogue safely? I don't know. In the months that followed, the journey was never discussed.

When we arrived at the synagogue we were told that the Rabbi of Cardiff had decided at the last moment to accept an invitation to represent the Chief Rabbi at the investiture of the Prince of Wales. He left a letter to be read out in his absence. My mother began to cry. Then, miraculously, my cousin, also a rabbi, who had married her all those years ago, took over. He walked to the Victorian organ and played, then sashayed in front of the organ to perform the marriage. The marriage ceremony was saved. My new husband gazed at me under the *chuppa* – marriage canopy – and I knew that all the fighting and arguing was worthwhile. I loved this man. He smashed the glass under his foot and the congregation shouted *Mazaltov*. We were finally married and allowed to kiss publicly. Then followed what seemed like a thousand photographs of smiling to order, while in the background my grandmother stood strong, still and unsmiling – a powerful lady with enormous influence. As the photographer clicked and darted about like some vast feeding bird, she scowled at all the fuss.

After the ceremony, it is customary to spend a few minutes together eating some cake. The bridegroom has fasted until that moment. Although the caterers served us cheesecake, which neither of us like, to be together and to be told that we should just relax, made this one of our most perfect experiences. I felt as if some of the sealed locks in my house snapped open.

After, it seemed, another thousand smiles and camera clicks, we climbed into the red Rolls Royce for the twenty minute drive to the reception. Totally alone at last. Just the elegant swish of a finely tuned engine in our ears. We wanted the journey to last forever.

When we reached Bindles, the reception venue, we found that somehow that clicking camera, feasting on smiles, had got there ahead of us. Here we had a group picture of my father's family, with my grandmother frowning in the foreground. Then a group shot with Mervyn's family, my father-in-law beaming with happiness at the one end and the father of the bride glowering at the other.

The happy couple with the bride's family

Most of the memories of my wedding day have faded. I do remember being kissed by many strangers and shaking hands and smiling and smiling for the ever-present photographer. I can't even remember the food that my mother so laboriously checked and listed – hours upon hours of crossings-outs and new lists. The whole event is a blur interspersed with whispers from my new husband:

'Five hours to go…four hours to go…not long now'

Such a terrible waste of money. But I still hope that somewhere in the cloudy miasma of that day, my mother gained some pleasure and happiness.

The M.C. dressed in his elegant red coat made a final announcement that the bride and groom would be leaving soon. I changed into a red mini coat and dress made out of bonded jersey. (I saved the outfit for years at the back of the wardrobe. I felt it represented my flag of freedom. But the bonding of foam disintegrated and showers of grey dust fell about the wardrobe floor and the outfit had to be binned.)

I hugged my mother and kissed her and my father gave me a superficial public twitch of his lips on my face and we ran out to our hidden car. We were on our way. Just the two of us. To spend a first night at Caerleon and then a flight to Malta, and on to Rome. It was all Merv's surprise, splashing out to make our honeymoon memorable.

The air in Malta was balmy with gentle breezes and a hot sun. We pretended we were lizards and lay on the rocks near the hotel and missed every breakfast with our loving. Just over two weeks passed effortlessly. We became spoilt by the easy ambiance of a place where pleasure was more important than time. I wrote postcards and pushed my daughter's guilt into the bottom of the suitcase.

Rome was a shock. In the middle of July it was a thirty-five degree city, thick with dust. Every corner buzzed with motor bikes like angry hornets, jabbing at the traffic. The humidity drained our bodies like a woolly vampire. Merv had booked a room for us, or thought he had.

The proprietor dressed in black with a white apron opened the door. Her face was creased with lines.

'Someone very sick is in there,' she snapped. 'They cannot be moved. We only have a small room at the back with no bathroom but you may take a bath in the bathroom at the end of the corridor, with my permission.'

She kept the bathroom locked. The keys hung about her solid waist on a thick silver chain as if she were a jailer. We bathed, removed city dust. It was instantly replaced by clammy sweat that ran down the backs of our just-washed necks encouraged by the closed heat of our small room which had no air-conditioning. After we used the bathtowels – no more than oversized tea-towels – we folded them and laid them in a small heap in the corner of the room on the bedroom terrazzo. Our jailer hammered on our door. We opened it quickly anticipating some terrible emergency.

'And where are the bathtowels? You've stolen them?'

'Stolen them? No, we brought them back into the bedroom.'

In the morning we paid our bill, offered quick respectful gazes of admiration at the Sistine Chapel, and then exchanged flights to go that day to London. We managed to find a room in high-season London and kept silent to our families that we had returned.

But an unspoken seam of anxiety ran through those last days of our honeymoon. Although they were blissful days, walking, eating sandwich picnics outside Westminster Abbey, cruising up the Thames to Kew Gardens, theatre visits and romantic suppers, reality was whispering in our ears, telling us that our perfect peace was nearly over.

It was time to return to our new home. We arrived very late in the evening and a painter and decorator was anxiously putting the finishing touches to our bedroom. By the time he left and we had cleared up his mess and I'd made us some supper, it was the early hours of the morning and too late to ring my parents. First mistake. The next morning I rang.

'Hello, Mummy, how are you?'

'Oh, you've remembered me. How was it on your honeymoon, away with him?'

'Mummy, it was wonderful. Malta was so quiet and we used to watch the sunsets and…'

'Yes, very nice and then what did you do?'

'We went to Rome…it was a bit uncomfortable – very hot and we had a bad room, so we moved on to London.'

'London? London! You were in London? For how many days?'

'Oh, three days. It was lovely. We did all the tourist things. We sat by Westminster Abbey. We went on a cruise boat. We saw Tommy Steele in a show – he was marvellous.' I babbled on unaware that the silence at the other end of the phone was bristling with hostility. I was suddenly aware of it. 'Mummy, are you alright?'

Her voice had curdled into a growl.

'You were in London for three days and you didn't think to ring us? You weren't concerned about me. You only thought of yourself.'

'No, Mummy, no. It wasn't like that. It was our honeymoon.'

How do you explain to a sick woman that a honeymoon is special? That lovers wish to spend their time sealed within a bubble of euphoria and romance and leave it perfect, away from the outside world for as long as possible?

'Mummy, I've rung you as soon as I'm back.'

I heard sobs on the end of the phone.

'I knew it would happen. Your father said, the minute you were with him, you'd forget about me.'

'Mummy, I'll be round this afternoon – Merv is coming home for lunch and then I'll walk over to be with you. I promise.'

'Yes, yes, I've heard it all before.'

The receiver was slammed down abruptly.

Merv arrived home for our first lunch home-cooked together. I had cooked him liver and onions in a rich red-wine gravy topped with fluffy parsley dumplings – an old family recipe and a particular favourite of my father's. I dished out his food. The smell was mouth-watering.

'I'm so sorry, love,' he said. 'But I can't eat this.'

'Why?' I asked. 'It's Dad's favourite. I've spent most of the morning…'

'I'm so sorry. I hate liver and I hate onions and I loathe gravy.'

I burst into tears.

'Look, love, it's only one meal.'

'Oh, it's not the stupid meal…it's… it's the…'

That first time set a pattern. I would try not to tell him that I had been upset by a remark and would blame something else as the cause, then hours later we would discover the real reason for my distress.

After lunch, I left for my mother's house laden with presents. I had carefully chosen a good silk tie for my father, far more than we could afford, and some cigars, and a delicate soft knitted wrap for my mother.

I pushed open the back garden gate: a rustic affair made out of thick-cut branches nailed simply together. The sun shone warm over the herbaceous border and a strong scent of phlox and stock floated over the lawn. My mother's day-bed had been pushed just beyond the French windows to take full advantage of the breeze and the dappled summer sun. She was lying out there with a sheet dragged over her tiny body. It seemed as if she had lost even more weight. Now, even the bones in her skull seemed prominent.

'Mummy, I'm so glad to…'

'Why are you late?'

'I had to make Merv's lunch – and before that I unpacked and did a load of washing and that takes ages without a washing machine…And then I had to walk to you… I came as quickly as I could.'

I looked at her face. It was as if I had been away for years. Within three weeks, the slivers of flesh that could have been termed 'cheeks' had almost disappeared. Transparent skin was pulled tight over teeth that seemed suddenly huge. Her body was board flat – so much so, that where the mass of her flesh and bones lay on the soft mattress, the shape seemed to dip rather than show any configuration. Up till then, I had tried to ignore those feelings inside me that were telling me that I shouldn't have married. And, stupidly, I'd been hoping that when I returned from honeymoon with my new status, a married woman, my parents would have a change of heart – particularly my mother. But they didn't. I don't think they even looked at their presents. Now, after thirty-five years, the guilt still slides and curves around my composure. There is never a day when I don't worry or blame myself for those last months. The pathetic second-generation badges of guilt – my fault, my fault. I should never have left home. I should have never married. Mea culpa.

We slipped into a routine where I would walk every afternoon to cook something for my father's supper, in between carrying my mother to the toilet or dealing with bed-pans and vomit bowls. But my status *had* altered in their eyes. I was no longer the sweet daughter who would do anything to please her parents. I had become a traitor and gone over to the enemy. My father was furious when I refused to look after my mother overnight when he was away, sleeping in my old room again. I was happy to do it now and then but not all the time. Newly married, I felt that that was wrong.

However we continued the charade of the Friday night supper with my parents. I would lay their table after having

173

organised the next day's food. Firstly I would lay the table with a white damask cloth and polished silver and freshly picked flowers from the garden, or, when the garden had no blooms, I'd bring a small bunch from a shop. Then I would lay two bought challot – festival bread – over which we would say a blessing with the addition of a little salt. There would be chicken soup which I'd prepared the day before, skimming off every bead of fat. There would be roast chicken, or beef, roast potatoes, peas, carrots and a large dessert to follow. My mother would toy with a little of the soup, pushing aside the slivers of chicken breast that I had slipped into her bowl, concentrating on the small amount of liquid. But even that would be vomited away within the hour, in front of us. The meal at my parents' was a gargantuan affair and, as Merv had always been a small eater, I would leave out indigestion tablets on the kitchen table in readiness for our return.

It is only now, recalling those sad times, and knowing my mother's desire for perfection, that I wonder what it meant to her to vomit in front of us and her very new son-in-law. As if vomiting was in the same category as sneezing or hiccupping, rather than something that is considered revolting to watch. Poor Mummy. Poor Merv – how he suffered every Friday night.

By now, the summer's warmth was being chased away by icy blasts. I managed to prepare the food for the final festivities after the New Year in their house and ours. I roasted chickens and a turkey, saving the giblets to make a rich soup. I roasted and boiled potatoes and made rice for us. I'd stewed autumn fruits – the very last few nectarines and the new season's Victoria plums with blackberries and a handful of damsons, and this thick syrupy compote became the base for crumbles and sponges. In between I followed the routine of caring for my mother and each time I visited

174

their house I prayed that she would recover and it would be soon. I never considered the possibility of her dying. But in our own married life, our situation was about to change forever.

We had decided to have a child as soon as we could. There were no magic blue markers in the seventies. Just a trip to the doctor's surgery or hospital with a urine sample and a few days' wait for the results. Much to my parents' disgust we had already changed to a new doctor, for we were looking for a person who was mother-and-baby-orientated and separate from my old life.

I visited this new young man. Sat in front of his desk. He looked up from a pile of papers. 'Want the pill, do you?'

'No, rather the opposite,' I said with all the symptoms of pregnancy buzzing about my body. An examination confirmed my status. Yes! We were going to be a family. I was convinced my parents would be as thrilled as we were; traditionally it's every Jewish parent's dream to be a grandparent.

It was a Friday night and I was making the supper in my parents' house; Merv would come over after work. My father had been particularly difficult, snapping and angry when I'd asked him questions.

My mother and I were in the kitchen together. I had to lift her on to a stool made comfortable with the addition of pillows and a rubber ring, for she still wanted to dish out the meal. Once the portions were dished – of a size that had been abandoned in my own house – we sat at the table.

'We have some news,' said Merv. 'Ruth is going to have a baby.'

Bless her, my mother was thrilled. She kissed and cuddled me, holding me tight with stick arms. I could hear her heart beating wildly in her chest like a trapped bird as she squeezed her ribby bones against my body.

'Darling, I'm so thrilled,' she said.

My father seemed to be pleased. '*Mazaltov*,' he said.

I relaxed. 'We're going to tell Gertie and Nay tomorrow,' we told them. My mother and I started to talk dates, and how it was when I was born and did she think she could still manage to crochet and my father found a bottle of warm champagne in the dusty back of a wardrobe and we drank some heartily. I saw my father's expression change after he had retrieved the drink, but I ignored it, thinking that it must be something to do with work or some other worry. Or just another mood.

We returned on the Sunday at tea-time. Outside, torrential rain and a howling wind accelerated an early darkness. I walked into the kitchen to make the tea. As I walked into the kitchen, my father stared at me angrily and stormed out into the lounge where Merv sat perched on the edge of the couch, anticipating the next row.

'Bloody wrecker,' he growled. 'You've really done the damage now! Haven't you?' He pushed past Merv and banged upstairs to his room, refusing to come out for tea. As usual, after the throw-away cruelties of my father's words, my mother spent the rest of the day and night sobbing. And the next day, and the day after, he continued to ignore us and our news. This performance lasted for two weeks. Finally, in desperation, Merv spoke to my grandmother and asked her to speak to him. She commanded him to come to her house, then rang us to say that he was there. When we arrived, he was in the back garden, furious, puffing cigarette smoke over the fence to the cows in the countryside beyond. She called him and he moved away quickly. Then she, a small, limping but tough woman, chased him around the garden, bellowing that he behaved himself at once.

'Gunter,' she cried. 'Come here!'

She waved her fist at him and pointed to the space at her side like a sheepdog trainer does with his dog. My father turned his head then walked meekly to her and stood at her side with his head hung low, while she continued to scream at him in German.

Trying now to understand my father's resentment of the situation, I suspect his attitude to my pregnancy had its roots in his hatred of the physical aspects of sex. And, of course, he had, till then, still wanted me to move back into the house and look after my mother. Now that possibility had faded away.

Despite a sickly pregnancy, I still walked to the house every day after lunch, or sometimes to make lunch. But paradoxically, as my body grew and I felt happier, my mother's health seemed to decline, despite my efforts. I'm sure the doctors would say that her body simply could not take any more abuse – that it had just given up – but I am convinced that she was missing those small extras that I used to filter into her daily food intake. If she had been sick, I would make her a light tea with lemon, but with half a morning-coffee or a Marie biscuit on the side. Half a morning-coffee biscuit is eleven calories. If I ate an apple, I'd say, 'Want a bit? This is really lovely,' and cut off a slice – maybe another ten calories. Like a nurse watching over a sick child, I'd try to make every snack count. And try to ignore the desperate desolation when she began banging her stomach to remove it all. The drum drum drumming –

'It hurts,' she'd say, banging and hitting with her boned fist to force out every scrap. But then, after a few hours, I'd try again. I'd never give up – a gruel made with arrowroot and fruit juice, a little soup that would stay and be digested, a quarter of a piece of toast cut into melba curls. And it must have worked because, for years, she stayed alive. But now she was without me for most of the day. I regret.

These days, after a lifetime's obsessional study of Anorexia Nervosa, and of the chronicles of those so-called survivors of the Holocaust, I know a little more. That the whole thing

177

went deeper – beyond my capabilities to assuage. The more my father ran away, the more my mother suffered. She was being left again – abandoned now by her husband. During the day, if he was home, he would be working. During evenings and at weekends, if he was home, he would spend every hour in the greenhouse caring for his African Violets and his prize begonias. She was the inside plant craving attention. She needed twenty-four hour companionship, not nursing. I had provided and fed that need. But, finally, I left that house. Her loneliness must have been profound.

Now, when my father left to go away on his regular stints my parents began to lean on the kindness of wonderful neighbours – one of whom was a nurse. They also employed a live-out housekeeper – a sturdy, firm woman who watched her charge, but could never give the love that I could. It would have been good to do the occasional night-shift, but by then I was tired. I could do no more. Also, my pregnancy was not simple. I suffered severe headaches and dizzy spells. But I continued to watch my mother, always there in the afternoons, and still convinced that she was going to get better. I still believed in fairy tales and the myth that everything would come good in the end.

April had come and my baby was expected, according to the doctor's predictions, on the eve of the Passover. The process of preparation for the Passover had always been followed by my mother and it was up to me to be her hands. She was meticulous, following every rule. Every corner of a house was cleaned of any scrap of food – searching for unleavened bread. Then once the house was immaculate, the cooking began. She would sit on her stool, layered with pillows, trying to support her body by holding on to the work top with shaking fingers. When she had supervised the entire preparation, I would carry her or lead her back to the lounge where she would fall back in her chair with exhaustion. I'd make sponges without flour layered with jam and home-made lemon curd. Layer cakes made out of matzo and a dark chocolate cream of cocoa, eggs, coffee and sugar. A myriad of biscuits and cookies, almond macaroons, cinnamon balls, coconut pyramids, Passover jam tarts, Passover strudel, prepared in the hope that someone would call and want to eat. I ran around her kitchen with my bump so large that I found every move an uncomfortable effort. My stomach and back ached so much with continuous contractions that twice we went to the hospital and twice, after an enema, I was sent home, once on my birthday.

Three weeks after the predicted date I discovered a trickle of blood running down the side of my leg. I phoned Merv. We both panicked. We had no idea what was happening. We rushed to the GP.

We sat in the waiting room and I, worrying that the blood was showing, balanced my ungainly body on the edge of the tweedy reception seats. When we eventually saw a locum doctor, she screamed, 'Get out of here... you're in labour...quick ...quick ...Go!'

We'd driven down to the doctor's surgery in our new car. Our old car – the sexy black and red little Viva – had been sacrificed for the solid reliability and carrying value of 'The Maxi'. When we reached the hospital Merv, normally an extremely sensible and competent driver, saw a parking space down a lane at the back of the building. He jammed the new car between an old van and a stone wall in an effort to reach that space. As he tried to pull back, the sound of crushed metal scraped through our ears. Eventually, he pulled the car free. An awful sight – our brand new car no longer pristine and shining but battered on both sides, a wall covered with paint and a damaged van, which we would have to pay for. After leaving a piece of paper with our insurance details secured on the windscreen, we raced into the hospital. They rushed me through the ghastly processes that were considered part of giving birth then – enemas, etc

179

– and with the memory of two or three anti-natal classes in my mind and the image of a gentle huff-puffing which seemed to constitute childbirth, we waited. And waited. Nothing happened.

'It's often like that on the first,' the midwife said. 'Just be patient.'

They sent Merv home – he was cluttering up the place. In the seventies, husbands in a hospital were a nuisance.

'Please, can I have something to eat?' I asked.

'Nothing at all – you may have to have a Caesarean Section. Try to sleep,' said a midwife.

What did that mean? Every time I had visited the clinic, they'd muttered 'good child-bearing hips', but their only investigative tool was a small funnel shaped piece of metal which they placed on my stomach to hear the heartbeat.

It was late evening. I lay on my own in a small ward, wrapped in muffled sounds. I could hear the far-off screams of a woman somewhere in pain, the clatter of tea trolleys, and the laughter of night nurses preparing food for themselves. I was starving, lonely and scared. The sister had given me a buzzer to use only in extreme emergency, and I was too afraid of authority to use it.

Morning arrived early in Glossop Terrace Maternity Hospital. I smelt tea and toast and even hospital coffee seemed tempting after sixteen hours without food, but the trolleys kept passing my door. An orderly walked into my room to change the water in my jug.

'Am I having any breakfast, please?'

'Don't think so, love, tell you what, I'll go and ask, OK?'

She left and the sister, whom I later discovered was famous for her tyrannical ways, marched into my room.

'You were told you will have nothing as they may have to do a Caesarean. The doctor will be along presently.'

She re-jammed the sheet across my trapped toes, muttering about the untidiness of patients, burst past the screen and out of the room. Apparently Merv phoned, so he told me at visiting time, but I was not given any message. I heard the clunk and squeak of the food trolley at lunch time. An image of mashed potatoes floated in and out of my mind with the mild contractions that stopped and re-started. I can cope with this, I thought innocently.

Eventually, a consultant arrived.

'We are going to induce you,' he said. He littered words about the room about 'the dangers of infection' and 'shouldn't leave for too long', and 'best thing' and within a short while a drip mechanism was inserted into my arm. I wanted Merv. I wanted civilisation. I needed to speak to people. But the effect of the drip took its course. I was now experiencing full-blown labour pains. On my own. No husband. No family. But when Merv arrived for visiting, he was told that he might stay. The low and increasing pains of labour forced their way into my back. I had now been in labour for thirty-six hours. The pains were regular and very painful, and I had an internal examination every hour.

I know now that the baby had turned and was lying breech. I was told nothing at the time. The modern way of keeping the patient informed is so much kinder. Seeing my panic and rising discomfort, Merv was allowed to stay on, but he was made to feel a bother. He rubbed my back and sneaked wine gums into my mouth when the nurses weren't looking, just so I could pretend that I was eating something. We were running into the third day. My fears grew. The gas and air were not helping and the nurses had administered seventeen pethidine injections into my thigh. I still have a dead muscle in that area. Finally, they sent Merv out of the room. No one told me what they were going to do. I felt as if I was cut from edge to edge, and I did have thirty six stitches internally and another thirty six externally. Then they began to use forceps. Eventually, a little six and a half pound baby with navy blue eyes was born. Her nails were long and she was covered in a layer of dark hair which I understand is normal for a late birth but, in my distress, I thought I had given birth to a werewolf. It was only later, after they bathed her, that I saw my beautiful child. It was early in the morning. After the pain of stitches inserted by a student doctor, I celebrated with my husband's sweet kisses. And following his speedy dispatch by the ever efficient sister, an egg sandwich arrived accompanied by a steaming hot cup of tea. Nothing has ever tasted so good.

Exhausted from my ordeal, I was placed in a ward with four other mothers. It was mid-afternoon. I anxiously watched the clock for Merv's return at six. Seven o'clock came and went. No husband. At quarter to eight, Merv burst into the ward looking flushed in the May heat. As I saw him I began to cry – all rational thoughts lost in exhaustion.

'I'm so sorry, love,' he said. 'But when I got home I sat in a chair and fell asleep. I woke up with a fright – it was six o'clock. I raced out, leaving my jacket with the house and car-keys in the pocket and then I had to break into the house.'

I was so grateful to see him and for once Sister was lenient and we were given an extra quarter of an hour. He had rung his parents and my parents to tell them that they had a granddaughter. The next day must have been a Sunday because there was afternoon visiting and my father was home.

Breaking the staff-sister's tenaciously enforced rules, my father burst into the ward during lunch pushing my mother in a wheelchair. I say 'my mother' but now there was little of the precious person I recognised. I watched the other women in the ward reel with horror as she was wheeled to my bed. This was a very old lady beating her fist in her lap her bones covered with blue-transparent skin dotted with red where once bloomed cheeks. Even I, who normally saw her every day, had a fright. The other women's faces were full of revulsion, as if they were staring at the living dead.

But her voice was still strong – still my mother's. And angry.

'You didn't...you haven't...not for three whole days...You haven't rung me!'

'But, Mummy ...I couldn't...I was in labour!' (There were no phones by the bed in the NHS hospitals in those days.) 'I've had a drip attached to me...I've been in labour...'

There was no point in telling her about the agony of the birth, the hours and hours that preceded it. Her mind was in her own world, fed by a panic-stricken husband and her own beastly voices of hunger. She no longer felt my love or realised that I cared for her, or that I was looking forward to sharing my new child's development with her. In that short time since I had last visited, just a matter of days, she had drifted irrevocably away from rationality to an ethereal world of potions and more potions and the overwhelming negatives of life – her stepping stone to the world beyond.

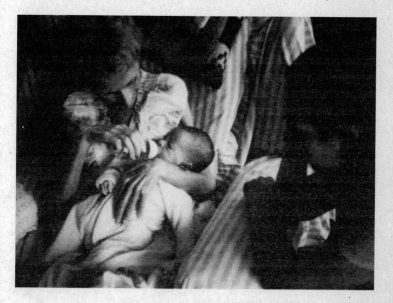

Judith cradling her granddaughter, Sarah

Chapter Thirteen

New Child Other Child

The baby needed feeding while my parents were visiting the hospital and we managed to balance that new, miniscule infant and a bottle in my mother's fleshless lap. She made an attempt to hold both, but her fingers were stiff and the child grew nervous and began to cry from the lack of support.

'She doesn't like me,' wailed my mother.

'She doesn't know you,' we chorused. But by then the sobbing was unremitting. It was impossible to bring her back to reality.

After the bottle fiasco my parents left the hospital. I never expected flowers or a card or a gift for the baby. But there were none anyway. That made the whole event even more poignant for, had my mother been well, or as she had been in the past, I know she would have come with flowers, cake and a teddy bear.

After ten days with no more visits from my parents, and an agonising infection in my stitches, I left hospital to care for my husband and my new child. Breast feeding was not easy. My baby wanted to be fed every two and a half hours. There were rules in those days that a child should only be fed every four hours. 'You must keep to a routine,' they said, and if you did not you would be doing untold damage. 'It is important for the child's health.' So, ever respectful of authority, I walked up and down the room with a starving, screaming child in my arms and one desperate eye on the clock. Hours and hours were spent pacing up and down trying to placate a baby who was so hungry that, eventually, after feeding, she would project the contents of her stomach across the room and then scream again. There seemed to be no one to ask. No one to talk to. I was suffering from post-natal depression, mastitis, cracked nipples, and a mother who said I was neglecting her.

In time, the lower infection passed and in a fit of inspiration, or maybe desperation, our child was placed on a new formula – from a bottle. At two o'clock in the morning, when yet again our baby had vomited her breast-feed across the walls and carpet, we telephoned a friend who opened his chemist's shop and offered us a new baby formula which worked! We had discovered by a process of elimination that my child was intolerant or sensitive to dairy products in my milk. Years later, I found that all those dutiful pints of milk and portions of cheese I consumed at this time were not the best foods for me or my child. I was equally as sensitive.

Nevertheless, despite all my own personal pressures, I still walked to my mother's house every afternoon, pushing the pram. I made her food. I carried her to the toilet, and scoured the toilet pan. I emptied her sick-bowls and, if she could not move, her bedpans. Often there was a full bed-pan waiting for me when I arrived, especially if my father had been absent for a while. I masked my own retching and then scrubbed up and returned to her side. I'd try to cook her tiny amounts of food to tempt her. I would make my father's supper and then leave. But by now most of my actions were met with verbal abuse.

'It is all your fault. If you had not married him, we would still be OK. You had to be selfish and think only of yourself…'

I'd go home and try to pretend that none of it had happened. I'd immerse myself in my other life of wife and mother, but the pain of those hours was wearing me down.

But I still had hope for my mother. I had lived for so long with the belief that one day we would discover a cure and that my mother would get better, that it had almost become a separate religion. Every Friday night, I stood at her side and lit a minute pair of candles next to her elaborate family candlesticks. Then with fingers over closed eyes, I would mutter the same words:

'Please, G-d, make Mummy better, and make us all a closer family, and please, please let them love Merv as I do. Look after Sarah and Daddy and all the family in Israel and let there be peace in Israel and in the world.'

Although my emotions were raw, and I still cried easily, we decided to have a party to celebrate our little daughter's birth and invite all the family. I tried to engross myself in the preparations. After all, if she had been a boy there would have been a ceremony, and we wanted our child to have her own special day and her blessing. I sat with guest lists and food lists. We had very little money or space and the only rooms that were free for visitors were our lounge and the tiny breakfast room. We decided to invite everyone for afternoon tea. More work, less money. I made pastry cornets which were later filled with freshly whipped cream. I made Welsh cakes, apple strudel slices, a honey cake and dark chocolate cake. On the day, I made egg sandwiches and a few open smoked salmon sandwiches which were then considered a huge luxury. Finally, we drove down to the local fruit market and bought a tray of peaches and a tray of seedless grapes and laid out a large platter of the fruit in the middle of the table. Half an hour before the visitors arrived, I dressed in the new outfit Merv had bought me for the party. It was a baby-pink brocade dress and jacket – probably not the best colour or style for someone still trying to lose extra baby weight, and suffering from embarrassment at the excess poundage – nevertheless, Merv was proud. He kissed me.

'It all looks great, love, and so do you.'

The visitors began to arrive. While the baby was still sleeping upstairs a crush of people developed in our small house. Cups of tea were being passed about and there was a wonderful air of celebration. I was pleased we had made the effort. Merv's parents were beaming with pride and then, at last, my own parents arrived. I opened the door. My father cast a disgusted look over my outfit.

'What on earth are you wearing?'

'Merv bought it for me.'

'How could you possibly wear…?'

I interrupted, afraid of a public display of aggression.

'Mummy, come upstairs and see the baby,' I whispered, thinking that if I separated them, then maybe my father would control his temper.

A slow process, but we managed to get her up the stairs. I sat my mother on our bed and brought the baby out of her cot to show her. She was dressed ready in her best.

'Yes, she's very sweet. But what do you think you are wearing?'

'Merv bought it for me. I had to have something instead of maternity clothes… and we found this in the sale… And I know Daddy didn't give it to me… but I loved the colour and…'

'You look like a couch,' she said. 'You've disgraced your father and people will think that he doesn't want to give you clothes.'

'But he doesn't…he says that he does but…he never…'

I stopped myself, afraid to say more. As I walked down the stairs with my baby, I felt that my new outfit made me look huger. That was the last time my mother visited my home

By now, fewer people visited my parent's house – just immediate family, a couple of friends and the doctor and housekeeper. It was as if the house's eyes had closed to the outside world. Almost as if the house was dying with its owner.

But then suddenly, when just *being* was so painful, my mother decided to write a children's book. It was the most wonderful miracle. The spirit of life was still strong. I was encouraged. She would be well again. She began writing with her thin claw hands in lined children's exercise books with blue biros and in a tiny script as if every line mattered. They were short stories about a boy called Bimbo and his dog. We talked about their purpose. To write how Bimbo gets into scrapes, and experiences the traumas that little ones live through in their first years: a first visit to the dentist, a stay in hospital, swimming in a large swimming pool. It was as if she was leaving a special part of her talent to us and, particularly, to her grandchild. Every day there was a new story. When I arrived she would read it to me with a glow in her eyes that I had not witnessed for a long time. Every phrase was carefully chosen, using small words that children could understand, yet coloured bright with imagination and sheer fun. She must have spent hours in the night writing, desperate to fulfil her dream of completing something lasting and perfect.

Weeks passed and, finally, the whole book was written. My father grumbled at the waste of money when she employed a typist to make three copies. Then, after a few advertisements in local papers, she found a local illustrator who worked in watercolour and high-lighted work in coloured inks – a little like she had occasionally done years ago. Gradually, over the weeks, a little boy with a tip-tilted nose and a mop of tousled black hair emerged, inspired by her words, and at his side was a mongrel with bright devilish eyes and wiry grizzled fur.

We didn't understand how publishing worked. We were told to 'send a dummy'. My mother glued the illustrations into a large file next to the text and began the research of where to send the book. She was exhilarated. The book was finished and I was so delighted with her progress.

The night we finished gluing it all together, I went home to my little house with my baby. I couldn't wait for Merv to come through the door. I busied myself making supper and, as he pushed the key into the lock, I rushed to open the door and danced about in front of him.

'At last, at last. I think I can see a bit of progress... there's a chance!'

It was a moment of perfect celebration.

The book lay finished in pride of place on a small table within her view, while my mother investigated further as to publishers and distribution. The good feelings about herself spilled over into other areas. She hankered for the days when she was involved in the fashion industry. She had always wanted to return to that life. Years before, she and my father had bought a shop on the outskirts of Cardiff where he sold the dress and coat samples from his business, and a little of the excess stock that was sold in the warehouse. Now she decided that she wanted sole control. Someone could drive her up there every day and she could run it. As she talked, I saw a little of the old light returning in her eyes.

There were moments now when we talked, when she was not sick. I would arrive and there was no nightdress. She had managed to dress herself down to stockings and shoes and a knitted cashmere suit with all the jewellery – rings, necklace and bracelet. Those days were golden. The shop was made over to my mother at the solicitor's with due formalities and with new dreams swirling around in her mind, she began to read copies of *Vogue* and *Draper's Record*. And wasn't she taking in just a little more food, or being sick just a little less?

I had my own proud announcement to make – we were going to have another child.

But a difficult pregnancy again, punctuated by severe backache, headaches and sickness. I had no car and washed all my child's clothes by hand as we did not have a washing machine either. At the beginning of the seventies, most women did not have all the labour-saving gadgets now

190

considered essential. So my free time became more fractured. I still visited my mother but perhaps did not see her deterioration. The ghastly was once again becoming the familiar. I did not see my father's steadied withdrawal. For even at that stage he was reluctant to let her take more control. Could he possibly have been afraid that she might return to her former strength, and oust him out of his places of safety and his other life? Did he still need to be king?

With hindsight I suspect he viewed any sign of recovery on her part as interference in his world. On the odd occasions when he was at home, he became even less interested in her. He disappeared more frequently. He cut himself off from her life in the house. He would gaze at the newspaper or the television as if her sad little routine of food, vomit, remove, food vomit, remove, her stomach cramps, joint pains, tears, were happening in another place and no connection with him. Mum would plead, 'Geoff, Geoff, what are you reading? Where have you been?'

But his guard would be permanently up. He would make phone calls in hushed whispers and I learned not to ask about them if I did not want to incur his anger. Mum was convinced he was seeing someone else. She used to tell me and I would always defend him.

'You must be wrong, Mummy…he would never.'

I watched him through her eyes, saw her go through his pockets, even talk to Merv about employing someone to watch him, but none of us could ever spell out our true suspicions. Instead, afraid of the truth we bumped about, hurting ourselves, in a fog of mistrust.

That new light in my mother's eyes began to die. I'd walk around to their house. She'd be dressed to impress him. But crying.

'It's hopeless… he doesn't care…you don't care… nobody cares!'

I was never able to console her. The book was shoved into a drawer. I wanted to give her more time but a growing child and a four and a half month pregnancy dragged my attention from her. Sometimes she would shout at me. It was weak but so effective.

'I've lost you. You're with him now. You don't think about me any more!'

And still my father stayed away. It was my responsibility, when I could manage, to go to the house, prepare flasks, lay trays. See that everything was in its place.

Maybe I should have stayed and slept there. I didn't recognise that the ending was so close. Mum had been ill since I was five and I was now twenty-three. But I felt that if I had taken that step I would have been manacled to their house. I was tired of giving, tired of loving with only hurt in return. I had placed my responsibilities to my own family ahead of those to my mother. As I sit and write this I am overwhelmed by guilt. It sits, as if it is another person about my body, clasping me, suffocating me.

It was a beautiful summer that melted into autumn. I felt hope for the future. As we stood in the synagogue during the New Year and the Day of Atonement, I still said my prayers that we would find the cure for what ailed my mother. Everyone else, I know now, saw that she was dying. Merv, ever loving, ever kindly, was keeping my thoughts buoyant to save me from worry.

'Yes, love,' he would still say, 'they could still find a cure – where there's life there's hope.' Small clichés of optimism like motes of sun in a darkened room. But the devils planned their final cruelties. The doctor had been called frequently during that month. I watched my mother go through the agony of excruciating cramps that would pull and disfigure her body. Apparently they were due to a potassium deficiency – her poor cells were crying out for a kinder balance. Now, the house echoed to her piercing screams. Then, one day, the final day, I arrived with Merv and a small parcel of food which was easier to prepare in my own home than in my parents' house. My father was home. His complexion seemed greyer than usual. I didn't notice Merv speaking quietly to the doctor. I was busying myself installing the food into the fridge for later. It was the eve of the festival of Shemini Atzeres – the end of the week of Succot, our beautiful harvest festival. I'd made bread, soup, salmon in sauce, a cake, and a liquidised peach and apple corn-flour pudding for my mother. I never read the clues. I'd missed all the signs. The doctor whispered to Merv to take me to the chemists for some ineffectual substance – just something to get me out of the house. He wrote a prescription.

'Love, we've got to get something for your Mum to make her more comfortable.'

I jumped into the car with him, pleased that the doctor had thought of something new. I am not sure that I had even seen her that day – her pain had become so much part of my dreadful routine, and putting food in the fridge was what I did to help. Is that terrible?

When we came back to the house, my father was bellowing like a wild animal and the house-keeper was crying. I did not know what was happening. My father growled and grabbed my waist-length hair, pulling me upstairs to my mother's bedroom. My mother was lying very still, her face twisted with agony and her eyes open. I had never seen a dead person. My mother looked so horrible. My father pulled my hair even tighter and pushed my face down on to hers.

'You killed her. You murdered her. If it wasn't for you she would still be alive. It's all your fault. You left her. You left the house – murderer!'

As he screamed I felt a strange tearing in my groin.

I sobbed, 'Not my…not my fault.' But she was staring at me with her unmoving eyes in her tiny wasted face. And I had not been there when she died.

My father was still shouting. Merv took the baby from the house-keeper.

'We'll have supper in our house,' he said. 'Come over to our house, this is not good for Ruth.'

When I returned home I noticed that I was bleeding. I said nothing. There were arrangements. I had to feed my baby and my husband and father. I muddled through like an automaton, all the time saying to myself: I wasn't there, I wasn't there. Ministers were informed and my father came for supper. But we couldn't bury my mother until after the festivities. The next day I walked about numbed. I cannot remember one moment, but I know the following day I attended the synagogue. We have a service called Yiskor. Its purpose is to pray for those who have passed away. It is serious and important. It is the custom in our town for those whose parents are still alive to leave the room. When they announced that they were going to perform that prayer, I had no idea whether I should stay or leave and there was no one to ask for help. I tried to speak to my neighbours but they must have thought that this pathetic blubbering person was to be avoided and ignored my frantic whispers. The cantor started to chant the prayer for the dead. I had never heard those elegiac melodies before. I stood sobbing, confused and embarrassed at my ignorance. Then quickly moved past the others and ran out of the synagogue.

I was still bleeding.

The following day, my father was expected for lunch but about an hour before his usual time of arrival, he stormed up our drive and through the back door to the kitchen. I was roasting meat and making gravy.

'Hi, Daddy, you're early…I…'

He threw a cream leather box – the size of a double shoe-box – at my feet. I recognised it as the box that held my mother's jewellery. Images of her face as she stared into the box to choose what she would wear that day, and those elegant hands touching, almost caressing, her treasures, crowded before my eyes. Wasn't she just in the other room after all?

'That's what you wanted,' he said. 'That's all you ever wanted!'

'I?'

'Just a scheme to get her jewels – well, you'll be happy now.'

He left and I sobbed and Merv quietly took the box and placed it in the safe. One day when the wounds were not quite so raw we would share the jewellery between her sisters and my children.

Later that day my father arrived for supper and, the day after that, they buried my mother.

In those days women did not attend funerals but waited in the house of mourning. It seemed sensible to designate our house as the house of mourning as my father was now with us. My mother-in-law helped me cover all the mirrors and the television with white cloths and, the night before, I found as many cups and saucers as I could.

The women began to gather in our little home. They were dressed in tweedy suits and dark hats and muttered in sombre tones whilst carefully looking for the most comfortable chair. We did not have very many pieces of furniture. All the time the pain in my groin was becoming more severe. I needed to sit down and there was nowhere. We must have been provided with the small low wooden chairs that were issued by the community for times of mourning but I suspect they had been mistakenly left at my father's house. The sounds of agitated women became louder. I knew I had to escape to breathe. Naturally the conversation focussed on my mother, and many of the questions picked at my discomfort.

'Ruth, what happened at the end?'

'How exactly did she die?'

The crushed heat in my little breakfast-room, decorated in psychedelic shades of red, orange and purple, became unbearable. By now, the pain in my belly was agonising.

'Must leave,' I whispered. 'I'll be down in a minute.'

But it was not bodily pain that prompted me to leave that space. I was simply overwhelmed by the events of the last days. I felt numb with loss and kept rewinding the scene of my mother's passing, even though it was torture. It was as if I had to go through the process – as if I had to hurt myself.

I made my way up the stairs to the relative quiet of the toilet and locked myself away. Horrified, I stared at a flood of blood pouring from between my legs. Suddenly, I was aware of what was happening. I stayed there as the pains increased for about an hour. Then a large substance tore out of me. I must have cried out. I heard a hammering on the door.

'You can't come in,' I shouted.

'Don't be silly,' said my mother's friend. 'Let me in!'

'I think I've lost the baby.'

'Where will I find the towels?'

'Airing cupboard.'

A slam of the cupboard door and I unlocked the toilet. She cleaned me up and got out my nightdress and put me to bed. Then she cleaned the toilet. In the meantime, Merv, grey-faced, returned from the funeral with my father and the rest of the men. The kind lady took Merv aside away from the general hurly-burly and told him that I had lost the baby. I will always be grateful that she was there for him when he cried.

Eventually, the throng left, the house became quiet, and the doctor arrived, telling me that I had to go to hospital. With so much loss surrounding us both, I did not want to go and refused, so I was ordered complete bed-rest for a week. No one talked of the baby that had gone. Although, later, Merv and I mourned the passing of our child, there was no public acknowledgement of our bereavement. Certainly at that time, according to the Jewish religion, as there had been no birth, and no life, it was just a lump of tissue.

We 'got up from Shiva' – finished the official mourning process for my mother – on Friday. We had the Sabbath to ourselves and then, on the Sunday, my father arrived with a lady guest and her grandchildren for dinner. Without warning, without invitation, I was expected to welcome this woman to our home. I was confused and very sick. I wanted to call him traitor, but in the end said nothing and even stood weakly for photographs with this stranger. And yet, despite all my efforts, my father was still angry. It was impossible, whatever we said or did, to placate his fury.

Gradually, my physical pain eased slightly and my father began to come regularly for evening meals. He kept asking me to visit my old home. I knew he had disposed of my mother's clothes, except for the furs, during the week of the Shiva so he really had no need of my help. He just wanted me back in the prison. But, already troubled by ridiculous fears and persistent nightmares, the idea terrified me. I was so afraid that I might stumble on a vestige of something that might jettison me back into my sickness. I had to stay strong, and visiting that house would not help.

Although my father had become progressively more difficult, I still felt that we might be able to build some sort of relationship together, if just for the sake of my daughter. Also, as an only child I tended to grasp whatever scraps of blood connection there were. Occasionally I let him help when I was bathing the baby, though I watched every move. He'd lift her out of the bath for me or put her on his lap and tell her stories and she responded, and every time I touched his loneliness.

Some would expect the story to end here. Judith has passed away and surely we are into another tale. But in fact my life is the same narrative evolving. I was part of the second generation who watched, tasted and absorbed their parents' lives and then began to *be* them. I inherited the legacies of my mother's sickness.

Furthermore, there is another aspect to this story which only becomes evident with my father's passing. It is then that the story is finally finished.

Chapter Fourteen

Bridge Over Troubled Waters

I was baking for the Sabbath. It was a bright spring day in 1971, so I'd opened the back door to the garden. The air was full of birdsong and I was feeling positive about the future. The doorbell rang – it was my father with some documents.

'Ruth, I need you to sign these now. Sign here, just sign here.'

He pushed a folded piece of paper towards me. I could see no other writing other than my name and some dots with a space to fill them. All the rest was hidden by the folding. I never hesitated. I signed them.

Two weeks later, I received an official-looking letter from a solicitor saying:

We are surprised that you have signed over the lease of the shop that was left to you by your mother...we have therefore been requested to ask if you will sign over the rest of that part of your mother's estate that was left to you.

I can remember screaming – sounds outside my body reverberating like cries from a wounded animal. I had thought that it would finish with the death of my mother. If my father had only asked me, I would have gladly signed a Deed of Variation. I had no need for a shop, with two very young children. But he had chosen to steal my mother's gift to me. She had planned and thought about what she wanted to do after her death. It was her way of telling me that she still thought of me and cared about me despite the last days. My initial reaction was to never speak to him again, and for a few weeks it was impossible to communicate with him. People would stop me in the street and ask, 'And how is your father now?' 'Do you see much of him…do the children…he must be a very lonely man.'

I felt as if I was at the bottom of a pond, trying to see out of the mud, sucking gasps of breath, frantically searching, scanning my father's wounding actions over so many years. I was in conflict with my religion, with those righteous rules, preached to me by priests and rabbis, of loving my father, respecting him and always being the perfect daughter. I knew that I could never treat my children as he had treated me. This final act for some reason changed my feelings for him forever. When he had abused me in the past it was just me. Now he had tarnished and spoiled my mother's final gift to me.

I have read accounts of others in such situations, and they terminate all connections. But guilt and anxiety forced me to reconnect. He was still my child's grandfather. He returned after a telephone call and after that brought his lady friend and her small grandchildren, often uninvited. I tolerated her presence, tried to be polite but choked in the kitchen.

On his good days my father would plead with me to visit the house. I tried to reason with myself; after all, it was just brick, stone and glass, but the fact was I could not even drive past the outside without reliving the pains. It was as if my mother's agonies and mine were trapped within the substance of the building.

I presume because of my refusal to visit, my father chose my mother's head-stone and the wording without discussion with me. The day the stone was set is dipped in dark shadows. I know I prepared food for the guests when they returned to our house. I know I was heavily pregnant and dreading the whole occasion.

When we arrived, there were crowds of people waiting to pay their respects – people who loved and remembered my mother. The dark-hatted chanting crowd mingled with family who had come from other towns. Whispered words of regret, tinged with guilt, hung in the air like invisible balloons.

'I should have visited more often…poor thing…they say that she was just skin and bone at the end…How old was she? Just forty-six! How terrible! I should have gone to see…But Geoffrey was always so…shush…not the place.'

I was afraid of the moment when the rabbi would pull off the black cloth that covered the stone and I would read the writing that placed her finally there in that cemetery rather than in my imagination. So final. So I tried not to see, not to hear. I looked at the grave stones about her. And then to get through the last moments I concentrated on the stony ground directly in front of my eyes. I heard the minister say, 'And the inscription reads,' but then had to stop the tears and ignored his words. We left and walked away. I turned my head and looked at where she was buried and saw my father had organised a vast black granite stone – more suitable for an eminent member of the community, not a dainty woman who loved singing, painting and friendship. But it was too late.

I went home and served the food: cakes I had baked in advance, her recipes of chocolate and vanilla marble cakeand heard the words of approbation and comparison.

'Lovely cakes, Ruth. They look just like your mother used to make. Yes, your mother was a wonderful baker – do you remember the time she made the Jerusalem Baby Home out of cake? She even made tiny little nappies out of rice paper and strung them on cotton lines. We auctioned it after and raised a great deal of money for charity… such a talented lady.'

Eventually they left, muttering kind thoughts and uncomfortable words of condolence. Like a brainwashed animal I went through the motions of making and serving a meal for Merv and my father. Something cold and quick. My father left and then there was just the two of us left downstairs with our thoughts and my mother's presence drifting around us as strong as perfume.

'I'm so upset,' I started. 'The stone...the colour...the heaviness...'

'*You're* upset?' he said, 'the wording – didn't you read it?'

'No? Should I...what is the matter?' I looked at his face and his grey cheeks.

'He left my name off the listing of the mourners...No, whatever you say. That was deliberate. Everyone is there except me.'

'You must have been mistaken!'

'No, I am not.'

In some religions I know it is the custom to write just a few simple words on a stone. But the Jewish religion requires a certain amount to be written in Hebrew and at that time it was customary to list close family including in-laws and grandchildren. To omit was to insult or deliberately hurt. It could be read that the person did not exist. Omission is often seen when families fall into dispute. Now the constant reminder of a hurt was indelibly carved into granite.

Chapter Fifteen

Birth and Afterbirth

Fortunately, within a few weeks of the stone-setting, our son, Jolyon, was born. The religious opinion was that this baby, by virtue of the time of his birth, would inherit my mother's soul. It was a beautiful and reassuring thought. He was a fine-looking child who arrived far quicker than his sister and a whole pound heavier at seven and a half pounds and was one of the longest babies they had ever seen at the hospital. In two days we were home and I returned to looking after my newly enlarged family. But a haze of depression clouded my days.

'Normal, my dear,' said the health visitor. 'It often happens – the readjustment of hormones after a birth and you had a bit of a difficult time before.'

The days passed. I felt physically ill, unable to move quickly, sloping from child to child with tiredness seeping like an insidious dust into my pores. I seemed to eat it, drink it, brush it off briefly for an hour or so when Merv and I were together and then, when I returned to my singular state, scoop it up and feel its poison once more.

'Don't worry, it often happens,' said the health visitor. 'You'll see, in a few weeks you'll be right as rain. A warm milky drink at bed-time does wonders. Now let's weigh the baby – my, he's a strong-looking little boy, isn't he?'

To the outside world I had recovered. I was good at smiling, always able to beam, masking my true feelings. A superficial glance would see that at last my poor mother was laid to rest, and I could rebuild my life, that I was a happy woman with a loving husband and a perfect, one boy, one girl, family. No one except Merv knew about the consuming nightmares that stamped over my quiet, shaking my body to fever pitch. Merv held me in the night and told me that they would go. And as long as I was with people, the devils held back.

We began to socialise like a proper married couple. There were people that I had known from my childhood and charity work and Merv's friends who were rather older and to me a little daunting. We visited, entertained as much as we were able to on a limited budget, with coffee and cake, biscuits and a cheese board, or bread and fruit, when we were short of cash. But as the finances increased, we began to follow the seventies trend of elaborate dinner parties. Everyone would be in formal dress, the ladies in long dresses. I would cut out and sew my own dresses late at night to keep up standards. The food followed trends set by our parents. So I spent hours cutting melon into balls with a finicky gadget, decorated canapés with tiny metal cutters to form slivers of egg white, cucumber and tomato peel into flowers – a tray for four could take hours to prepare. Beef Wellington – beef in pastry – home-made water-crust meat pies and pâtés all took time to prepare. The most daunting recipe I ever created was a boned-out turkey filled with a boned-out chicken, filled with homemade pâté and sausage, olives, capers and pistachio nuts, and the whole then sewn together to remake a semblance of a bird which, after roasting, was given a head and wings in puff pastry attached by copious amounts of mashed potato. All these party preparations were additional to the elaborate food I prepared just for Merv. I would make my own bread in the morning so that his sandwiches were as fresh as possible. Then I'd walk into town with the double pushchair to deliver his lunch. He'd come home in the evening to Plaice Bonne Femme made in a light sauce garnished with peeled green grapes and swirls of piped duchess potatoes followed by homemade apple tart, when, if the truth were known, he would have preferred a macaroni cheese and a bunch of grapes.

And our small house had to look perfect. I was super-meticulous. My mother had set the standards and they were right. I was trying on her high-heeled stilettos of perfection, slipping my feet into their entrapping restrictions, and pulling the straps tight about my ankles. Twice a day all the carpets were brushed by hand with a dust-pan and brush. The children's toys were organised every night into their respective boxes and then perfectly arranged. I would make all the children's clothes. This was partly because children's clothes were so expensive and I wanted my children to look as good as their friends, but also it kept me busy – occupied. As soon as the little ones were in bed, I took out the sewing machine that had been my mother's and was only loaned to me, laying it out on our sitting-room table and used a large cutting-out board on the sitting-room floor. I cut out party dresses, and trousers and shirts, and even a coat made out of soft pink wool to make my children the smartest children in town. But it was not showing off. The whole process gave me a raison d'etre. And the clothes were so carefully made that later I was able to sell them and recoup enough money to buy more fabric for the next sewing session. So I could even justify the process. It made me look capable, thrifty – the perfect housewife.

But Merv was afraid to move, let alone relax, in his perfect palace and often when he returned from work exhausted he just wanted to eat a piece of bread and cheese. Although I was busy, very, very busy, my head was spinning with anxieties. I tried to run a less restricted house and thought I might spend time with neighbours, like others did, enjoying that pleasant process of leaning over the fence or sharing a coffee at a kitchen table. But our neighbours were elderly and uninterested in a young family with babies. I would walk miles with the pushchair just to run away from myself, or at least my thoughts.

While I was away from the house, I was away from the chattering fears that invaded my space. With the door shut and me inside, the walls began to merge together, squeezing and suffocating me. I suffered from acute loneliness combined with irrational fears. With hindsight I can understand why. For years every waking moment had been programmed. From the age of eleven every second had been as dedicated to keeping my mother alive. Now the hours stretched out, unstructured, and I had two small babies and no adult company. Just an irrational clock that would slow down in the evening before Merv's return and race on a Sunday for the few hours we were together. I did see friends once a week, but they also had small children and the conversations revolved around feeding, nappy-rash and bed-times. I craved good conversation and quality discussion. And SOMETHING ELSE! I was trapped in a web of babies and babyhood. The situation was aggravated by Merv's late hours. He was ambitious and concerned to be the best provider. So he worked a full day in Cardiff and then three afternoons a week he would travel an hour out of Cardiff and take a late surgery in the valleys. When he returned home he would be exhausted and so would I.

I loved him desperately and felt I was only alive when he was there. I wanted him to talk and tell me every minute detail of his day, but he yearned to shut it out and relax. It was evident that I had to find something else in my life. I could feel myself in dark surroundings, as if I was slipping down a black shale-covered slope. Sometimes it felt as if the ground beneath my feet was actually shaking, and would drop me into a chasm. I became nervous of walking down the stairs in case I fell. There had to be a way back to normality.

I sat in our doctor's surgery and aimlessly flicked through an ancient magazine. A small cartoon made me chuckle and I asked if I could pay for it, took it home, cut it out and began a collection of jokes that helped on the tough days. I also began to enter competitions and win. I was cheered by the thought that the post might hold a little excitement rather than just bills and looked forward to starting the day with a reward rather than a blank.

But these tactics couldn't totally offset the grim. The structure of our days remained the same. I was at home with two babies and very little money and a husband who had a miniscule amount of free time – just late evenings and a Sunday afternoon from two-thirty until five-thirty, when it was time to start the baby's supper and bath routines.

It was not enough. Visions of my dead mother plagued my days and nights and there was no one apart from Merv I could talk to, but it felt unfair to spoil his life. He knew about the nightmares because often he would have to wake me and hold me as I sobbed, terrified, in the dark. I could not pluck up the courage to talk to my friends Somehow it would have felt as if I were losing face. Everything should be perfect after marriage. I was locking in my secrets – my mother's dangerous tradition.

One Monday evening the children were sleeping in their cots. They had been particularly awkward, as children are if they know that their mother is tired. I had spoken to my grandmother who had been irritable and my father had visited and been unpleasant – no more than usual, but it all had a cumulative effect. I had tried the jokes, the competitions, a new recipe, but I could no longer see past the painful vacuum of loneliness and terrors. I sat in our small colourful sitting room, flipping the channels on the television. But the seven o'clock game shows could not hook my attention. I had a mug of tea in my one hand and a small apple in the other – delaying my meal so as to eat with Merv.

Maybe if I move a little, I thought, think up some chores to do…there must be something…there's always something…I might just chase away the bad. Forcing myself out of my chair, I walked around the house aware of my breathing, and of a faster chasing heartbeat. I picked up and studied the ornaments we had bought together, trying to bring to mind the special times when we discovered them, hoping that they would pull me back and re-establish a sense of reality, by recalling our good times. But it was as if all this was outside of me in another space. I felt enclosed in a bubble of terrors.

I slipped into the children's rooms; they were both asleep. I tucked in their covers and kissed them both and listened to their soft sweet breathing. Even the sight of those little ones with their golden curls did not smack my consciousness into some kind of sense.

A good bath and a hot drink will relax and use some time, I thought – the old magic trick. I walked slowly into the bathroom. By now I was trying to fight off a severe migraine.

A couple of painkillers to go with the drink, I thought.

I opened the locked bathroom cabinet and took out a bottle of painkillers and stared at the brown glass – almost a full bottle left over from the time of the miscarriage. My heartbeat pumped faster through my chest and juddered through the whole of my body.

Better in the bath, I thought. By now the drink was cold; nevertheless, I placed it next to the bottle of tablets, and undressed carefully in the bedroom. I hung up my clothes and slipped slowly into the water and felt the warmth slide around me. I was mesmerised by the sight of that brown bottle and its enchantment of finality.

I must have lain there for hours, staring at the bottle and the drink. The water turned to ice-cold. My thoughts were paralysed, yet racing madly. My whispering devils suggested that the whole bottle would be such an easy peace. But there was something that held me back, kept me lying in the cold, motionless. Barely breathing.

Outside the bubble, I heard calling. It was Merv. Getting no response, and used to my face at the door as he arrived, he ran up the stairs, burst into the bathroom, saw me, the tablets and the drink, and realised immediately what had happened. As I saw his face, the frightening spell of the tablets was over. He yanked out the plug and, grabbing a towel, he pulled me out of the icy water. He held me until we had both stopped shaking. We held each other, sobbing. He smoothed my back, kissed my face and the sides of my neck. His face was twisted with sadness. Then he helped me into a nightdress and dressing-gown and we went downstairs and ate what was heating up in the oven – neither of us tasting the lovingly prepared meal. The abyss was still so close.

After supper I told him of my fears and, later, in bed, he held me again. There were tears in his eyes.

'I promise I'll find a way,' he said. 'We'll get you some space from the kids and I'll try and cut down my hours, I promise I'll try.'

He did try. He phoned me in the evening if he was going to be late and we found a lady who would have the children for two afternoons a week so that I could have some rest. I now had one free afternoon when I could make the children's clothes without worrying that they might hurt themselves on a stray pin or a pair of scissors. We told no one about that night. But the memory of it hung like a spectral film over our equilibrium.

We were still trying to *'keep sholem'*– keep peace – with my father, despite his efforts to provoke arguments. For the sake of the children we wanted to maintain a relationship. But it was always difficult, and our efforts were rarely appreciated.

Now my mother had died, my grandmother had reassumed the matriarchal power within the family. She was elderly now and physically weaker than she had been, but seized her crown with enthusiasm and insisted that her family kept the strict rules of duty and obligation. When I was preparing my father's food a small basket of goodies was laid out to take to my grandmother which my father and I would deliver.

She lived with her own devils. She had lived on the East German border, always subject to invasions. As a young girl she had seen the Cossacks setting fire to her village. She witnessed pogroms when Poles, resenting the Jews, raped and pillaged their small village. She had been part of events in the concentration camps that thank G-d I have only read and dreamt about. Very infrequently she would talk about times in the camps – mainly the starvation, relishing the story. She would make me cry. I'd try to blot out her words, look at her and try to reason, but the small lady with the scarred face and the limp who paced up and down her sitting-room bestowing chocolates to my family – always before a meal – held the reins of guilt and fear and tightened her grip with her lectures. When I left her house, I'd try to forget her German language, the constant reminders of duty and obligation that she would try to force on my shoulders: that I should visit even more frequently, that I should take food for friends of hers who had come out of Germany and were now on their own. I would visit her a few times a week to take her food, replacing the preparations I'd made for my father and which he had reluctantly delivered. The regimes of the concentration camp were instilled in her and she would only eat the old food when I had brought fresh – always keeping a reserve safe on the cold glazed tiles of her larder. I have seen her cut the mould off a piece of Madeira cake and eat it and then ridicule my discomfort.

'It's good food – you must not waste it,' she'd whisper, with a bang of her stick on the immaculately cleaned carpet.

But sometimes she would not want to eat. She suffered from loneliness, often depression, and had to be persuaded frequently. I devised a method to encourage her by bringing my children's tea to her house and cooking it there. She would sit with them as they ate and enjoy their company. I always prepared too much and, rather than waste it, she would eat what was left over.

My father was by now seeing another woman seriously. I had no idea who this lady was. He told me that she was an allocator for the same fashion house that he ran in Cardiff.

I tried to be happy for him. He was a relatively young man to be living alone without the companionship or love of a woman. Eventually we met her – a difficult and awkward process. Their relationship grew and finally we persuaded him to ask her to be his wife. To demonstrate our friendly intent, I offered to cater the wedding.

We wanted to give them a special present to commemorate the day. They already had a well-established home with Persian carpets on the polished floors, paintings, a collection of Swedish and Mary Gregory glass, and art-deco lamps, and we could not buy anything in that category. Nevertheless we spent days searching for just the right thing. Eventually, after a lot of discussion and a meeting with an antique dealer friend, we found a set of antique silver coffee spoons still in their original box. I wrapped them, delighted with my purchase and we presented them to my father and stepmother-to-be.

She opened the box and exclaimed, 'Rub a dub dub! Don't want to spend my time polishing these.' And handed them straight back to me. We still have them shining in their navy padded box.

They planned a grand wedding with the reception taking place in our house; we were to welcome all her friends and family. Forty people for a sit-down dinner –we opened the dining room and lounge into one large room. Simply organising the tables and hiring chairs and kosher dishes was a monumental task. I made a three-tier wedding cake with royal icing and curved trellis hearts decorating the sides.

On the day, the religious ceremony in the synagogue was marred only by the cries of a small child. The joke bubbled around the room that my father had to get married.

A gargantuan feast followed, as requested. Melon balls with blackberries saturated with Kirsch sat in frosted martini glasses. Traditional chicken soup was served in large bowls with a choice of *knaidlech* – dumplings – or *lockshen* – noodles. Most people had both. Roast chicken and roast beef with potatoes and vegetables followed, and then I wheeled out a trolley with a choice of nine desserts. There was spiced sultana and apple pie, lemon meringue pie, a Black Forest gâteau, poached nectarines, chocolate Swiss roll filled with fruit and iced with bitter chocolate, a trifle, a Danish gâteau, a chocolate mousse and a vast fresh fruit salad. One gentleman asked for a soup bowl and ate a portion of each one.

When we look back on the day now, we remember the block of frozen soup which, when we tried to put it back into the saucepan, we found had expanded and would no longer fit and we were confronted with an iceberg of frozen soup laden with carrots and celery that had to somehow be served in a few hours. I still laugh when I think of Merv stamping and jumping on the polythene in an effort to force it into the pot.

I made myself a 'fashionable' dress which was black with a high neck, a panel of lace down the middle, and leg-of-mutton sleeves. When it was completed I looked like the house-keeper. I think many thought I was. We used so much power that the lights fused many times over the day. But everyone was fed and satisfied.

The new step-relationship was hard for me. Maybe my mother's presence was too strong. I could still not go back into that house. If I just went up the gate or stood outside on the path, I would feel her presence as if she was next to me. And it was not a happy presence. It was the presence of an

212

angry, tormented spirit who needed peace. I felt her pain so acutely that I could not bear to be near. I wondered whether it was my own reaction to her death: the ongoing guilt that trammelled my mind and my spirit. But I avoided that area of the town and remained afraid to return to the cemetery. My father constantly nagged me to return to the house. 'There are no ghosts for me,' he said. And yet I had never mentioned the word 'ghosts' to him.

My father and his new wife travelled to exotic destinations like Rio de Janeiro for the carnival and I hoped they would enjoy their life together. But he appeared to become more nervy. He had completely changed his diet, existing on red meat and oranges to reduce his weight, combined with continuous caffeine-loaded cups of strong coffee. During their lives together, my mother had persuaded him to cut down on his cigarettes and cigars, but in his new life he seemed to be smoking even more. Now his new wife would carry a spare pack in her handbag, which she shared with him. He was never without a white tube in his mouth and he coughed more than before, spitting into a white handkerchief or, more disgustingly, on to the pavement. Furthermore, his temper was not improved. His level of tolerance was now at a point that could be broken by the slightest pressure.

But in my own home things had changed for the better. The house ran at a faster pace. I now had my own catering company which had started when I was asked to cook for a farmhouse shop. I made tea-flavoured fruit loaves and they would sell well. But there was no real satisfaction in the labour. Then I entered a cookery competition and was Welsh finalist for the Cook of the Realm, cooking in the final at Drury Lane Theatre. The late Roy Castle was one of the judges. I remember him tasting my food that had grown cold in the wait. After that the work seemed to flood in and, still hungry for more work, I grabbed an offer from Cardiff's major store, James Howell, where Merv worked. They needed a pâtissière. On some items I made a farthing profit. But it didn't matter. I was busy and active and involved in the outside world, and it kept the devils away. My father commented, 'You'll be taking in washing next.' I ignored his words. I also catered weddings parties, dinner parties, christenings, in fact all celebrations. I even catered a wake! The work kept me in the house with the children where I felt I needed to stay, but also kept me active.

I became the White Rabbit – very, very busy – watching the clock, stretching my time, trying to eat sensibly, running to meet the children from school. But, without realising it, starting to tread the path to thin that my mother had measured and paced before me. So I was up at five in the morning to begin baking, and the scent of fresh sponge and rising doughs would wake my family. Then one child to school and one to nursery and time for another two doughs.

Each week, just for the store, I made thirty-nine dozen fancies, ten gâteaux, and a change of the dessert trolley every day. My flour was delivered in sacks by a mystified delivery man who padded through my house leaving white footprints on the floor. The first time he called, he turned his head and exclaimed, 'This is the strangest bakery I've ever seen.' I lived on the spin of pints of black coffee and a fridge full of green apples. My hands began to itch with the constant water use and an allergy to the flour and my shoulders ached, but I ignored my body's complaints.

Weekends, I would be cooking for functions: small weddings, private dinner parties, intimate dinners for two when anxious husbands wished to impress, corporate cocktail parties and pre-rugby feasts. Food was prepared in larger and larger amounts. Sixty Christmas cakes, Simnel cakes at Easter, Danish Gâteaux, birthday cakes, tins of Florentines and shortbreads, jars of my own mayonnaise, and packed hampers to take on the beach. And still it was not enough. By now every finger was covered with plasters and underneath the plasters the fingers were black and septic. A consultant dermatologist diagnosed a flour allergy and ordered me to stop using my hands, but of course I couldn't.

One bank holiday I was catering two functions on the same day. An '*ufruf*' – the celebration of a new bridegroom, the week before a Jewish man is married – and a silver wedding. Ten large salmons sat cooling in their rich liquor, waiting for attention. Stacked boxes of vegetables jostled for importance.

In the early hours the salmons were laid on glass shelves and decorated with flowers – tiny petals cut out of egg-white and centres of carrot, using tiny cutters inherited from my mother. Long stems of cucumber skin curled down the length of the fish with twisting tendrils of pimento enhancing the shape. Next to them lay the salads: carrot and orange, heavy with sultanas, cucumber and tomato studded with olives, potato with rich homemade mayonnaise, spicy curried rice and vegetables – very avant-gard and always a hit with the men – green lettuces washed and bedded on platters to receive hard-boiled eggs, and platters of traditional chopped fried gefilte fish with their crescents of lemon and frills of parsley. In the freezer, lay two massive apple pies – exact replicas of the pies I made with my mother. I'd also whipped a billowing sugary quadruple ration of meringue and set it on top of four vast dishes of buttery crumbs and sharp, homemade lemon custard, and finished the chocolate sponge bases with whipped cream, thickened juices of black cherries and kirch, to make the seventies icon – Black Forest Gâteaux. I finally crawled into bed, stiff and cold, at seven o'clock in the morning.

'You alright, love?' Merv asked. I edged my chilliness over to his warmth and he held me.

'You pleased, love? Go well?'

And I snuggled into the comfort of his strong arms about my body, thinking that in a couple of hours I'd be calling for my waitresses and serving all that food, which would be gone in seconds.

But the catering was not enough. I needed to be busy all the time. I could be asked to cater four functions in two weeks but then have nothing for two weeks and that created difficulties in buying ingredients and booking staff. I was trying to introduce some kind of balance to my labours. I know now, with hindsight, that catering is always an ebb and flow of crazy times and quiet.

I contacted a local glossy magazine to insert an advertisement. The editor came to our house. I had just completed a very special birthday cake for a special client. The brief was 'something extraordinary' – I had created a fairy-land in cake. Tiny coaches of a minute train carrying a vast number of candles puffed around the edge of a confectionery landscape that was dotted with liquorice-timbered thatched cottages, the thatch made out of slivers of Shredded Wheat. When the editor saw the cake, he decided to send a photographer and asked if I could write a cookery feature as he was looking for copy. I could have the advertisement as my payment. After the first feature we came to an agreement that I would write in exchange for advertising. I loved writing. Loved placing just the right word on the page to capture a season, or scent or taste. It felt like painting pictures, as an artist lays down paint with a brush.

At the same time, my catering business was about to take a severe downward turn.

I had agreed to cater a wedding for sixty people – usually my favourite number. The order included the cake, the food to be delivered to the bride's home on the day of the wedding, table decoration and provision of the waitresses.

When the mother of the bride arrived at my home, she appeared to be extremely agitated, clasping and unclasping her hands.

'And will it be fine …and will we…?'

I was soothing. 'Everything will be lovely. Look at my photograph album…read the thank-you letters from my clients, pictures of the food. I've never let anyone down.'

'You are sure?

'Yes, I am positive – everything will be lovely.'

Unconventionally, she rang most days, and most weeks visited the wedding cake to offset her anxieties. She would sit in front of the cake and stare at the fine lattice roll-outs that lay on the rolling pin, and check each minute hand-made rose. It was a difficult situation for me.

Then there was a succession of disasters. A few weeks before the wedding, her husband was taken into hospital. The week before the function, two of the bridesmaids were taken ill with food poisoning. And two days before the wedding, the bridegroom was involved in a car crash. The poor lady could not cope and rang me for hours just to talk. And then we had our own disaster. My dear sweet mother-in law, who had been fragile ever since I met her, had suddenly become very ill and was rushed into hospital. I had to be near. I was faced with an impossible situation. The night before the wedding I stayed up all night and when a navy dawn streaked with grey arrived in a flood of birdsong, all the food was ready to be delivered. I paid a manageress to serve the food and the wine and hoped that she would not let me down. Any money I would have made disappeared in a welter of anxiety and payments for extra staff.

And as my poor mother-in-law lay dying, the wedding ran its course. Merv and I looked at each other

'No more functions,' we said. The whole episode had just been too traumatic.

Now, with my wonderful mother-in-law gone, it was essential to look after my father-in-law and make him as welcome in our house as possible. He would stay for hours. He was living our lives rather than his own. It was as if he had lost the will to live.

My professional world now moved into writing. The post of features editor for the *South Wales Spectator* became vacant and I wrote a cookery feature, a wine and dine page under the by-line of 'The Gregarious Gourmet' and other copy written under a pseudonym. In my free time I rewrote *Holiday Haunts for Great Britain,* updating an old-fashioned type of book to appeal to a modern traveller, and then began to receive commissions from various magazines to devise diets for the burgeoning surge of get-slim-quick addicts. I wrote the 'ice-cream a day diet' to carry the slimmer through her holiday, the Mars Bar diet, the chicken diet. I was an expert. I did a string of personality interviews for *Slimming Naturally* – a magazine that no longer exists. It was fun. I met Susan Hampshire, Richard Briars, Keith Michelle, Maureen Lipman, and many others – true professionals and all utterly charming. And the late Frankie Vaughan gave me my first interview and became a very dear friend – he and his wife were a privilege to know.

I was busy and should have been happy. But the devils still stoked me with fears, watched me stand on the scales, counting out the calories, measuring my reflection, pulling at imaginary pieces of flesh, examining my stomach for flatness, wanting it to rest concave and low between exposed hip-bones. And despite the constant activity in my life, I was lonely. We had moved to a larger house and there was more space. The children were in school all day and apart from when I saw my father-in-law, the house would echo with nothing. I still felt the walls slide together, as if they could crush me. The sensation was physical and frightening. Desperate to find a solution, I wondered about having a dog. I was home most of the time, we had a very large garden, and the children and I had wanted a dog for years.

The need for a dog grew. Images in my mind of Whiskey, the little golden cocker spaniel that I had had briefly as a child, crowded my imagination. An address was found and we were presented with a shoe box containing a golden silky fur bundle with ridiculously long eyelashes and elongated ears. We all loved her instantly and called her 'Lovely'. By that time, to add to my labours, I had a small antique business on the third floor of a large building. As it was on the third floor, with no lift, there were not many customers, so I was able to write in the quiet – which was most of the time. I walked the dog in the morning before I left and then raced home to walk and play with her before collecting the children at school. She munched her way through the layers of decoration on the walls but we all loved her and, as I opened the door, there she was welcoming me. Gradually the devils in the house were banished by her high-pitched barking.

I remained very thin; I would be navy-suited in the style of the active London-focused journalist, travelling on the train to discuss commissions and working for magazines. When I stepped off that train and arrived in London holding on to a slim briefcase, I felt vital, important not just someone's wife or the children's mother, but my own person, valued for my abilities. However I still lacked self-assurance. I pretended, wearing my mask of confidence, when facing those in the real world. I still wanted, needed my father's approval. I remember pushing an article under my father's gaze when I had a particularly large by-line.

'Dad, Dad – look at that. Look, it's in *Woman's Own* on the beauty page – a whole section written by me!'

'Yes, yes, very interesting. Merv, I'm thinking of changing my car. I've never been very happy with this one and the boys at the garage said...'

My stomach crumpled at his indifference. Still, I was used to it. What was hardest to bear was that his lack of interest extended to our children. They did not exist in his life. One of my saddest realities. For the first few months of my eldest child's life, he had appeared to be paying attention, but as soon as our son was born, he detached himself from the role of Grandpa. (As a hugely proud grandmother of two wonderful children, and so delighted to be involved in their growing up, their birthdays, their good and bad times, their first days at reception class, first ballet, swimming lessons – each imperceptible moment marking the daily progress of their lives, I find it impossible to comprehend.)

'Why won't he care for the kids – why, when they are so lovely?' I'd cry to Merv when they were asleep. I kept comparing my father-in-law's reaction to the children. How they had always been adored. How Nathan would slip them a white paper cone of sweets behind my back and I'd pretend I didn't see, how he'd ask if he could take them to the swings and slides and come back exhausted, falling into a chair and mopping his red face when they had run and chased and he'd tried to keep up with them. I'd watch his beaming admiration of a new drawing, pride in a good result in school. Most of all, he'd show his love.

Rejection became an integral part of my father's relationship with me and my family and sadly this side of our connection seemed to intensify after his marriage. On one occasion I had gastro-enteritis and had been ordered by the doctor to go to bed. Merv was able to take a few hours off in the morning but he had a full appointment book in the afternoon and evening. In desperation he phoned my father.

'I wondered if you could possibly…just for the afternoon…Ruth is so poorly, please do you think…'

'Think what!'

'Do you think you or your wife could have the children for the afternoon?'

'Neither my wife nor I are baby sitters,' he spat.

That was the only time we asked them to look after the children.

I spent that day wrapped in a blanket, hugging my belly and trying desperately to disguise my hurt from my children, realising that my father did not care for me at all, and neither did he care for my children. This event, so acute in my memory, initiated months of clinical depression. My sickness was quite severe. I felt bruised from the inside. I was embarrassed, shocked and very, very sad. I sat for hours in a chair staring out of a window at the world outside, not wanting to be part of it. I would see to the children, smile at Merv, make food for the family but it was as if my place had been taken by a doll wearing my skin: an unthinking doll, robot-like, performing the functions of mother and wife but without a heart or emotions. It was almost as if something had died inside. I was already mourning my father's passing.

I suspect that if I had not been Jewish and the power of family had not been as strong, we would at that stage have abandoned our connections with my father and his new wife. But the Jewish culture is powerful. The voice of the Jewish holidays, which punctuated our calendar, would insist that we visited the synagogue. I felt the power of the command to honour my father and my mother and felt manacled by duty. We went to the synagogue even though it was possible that my father might be present and I was always terrified of a public row. I had seen my father explode in front of others many times. Merv and I just wanted peace.

Also I was still coming to terms with my mother's death, and felt that she would have never forgiven me if I abandoned my relationship with my father. So, despite the pain, we would still try to welcome him and my stepmother at home. There would be some kind of vague truce which lasted no more than a day or two. They would come for the festival meal. I would take hours to create something that he enjoyed. Sometimes the ceasefire would last no longer than the beginning of the meal. He would walk out of the meal perhaps during the family prayers which always preceded celebratory food. More often than not he would criticise the menu. Usually, by the next day, he had found fault with the children's upbringing or their manners and would want to fight again. Still we kept trying for the children's sake and because my father was my father

The first night of Chanukah and the week before Christmas, Joe was seven and Sarah, eight. I rang him.

'Hi, Dad. Please will you make friends and come round and be part of the family? We so want to see you.'

'Yes, I'm bloody sure you want to see me.' Sarcasm dripped like mucus down the phone.

'Really, Dad – just come over and see the kids – after all it's Yomtov. It's Chanukah!'

Joe – over-excited and laughing– picked up the phone.

'Hi, Grandpa, has Father Christmas been down your chimney?'

The receiver was slammed down and the next thing I knew my father had arrived, fingers jammed on the door bell and screaming like a possessed animal. Merv opened the door. I came out into the hall. I had been putting the Chanukah candles ready on the menorah after preparing a special supper with traditional foods.

My father stood, eyes blazing, red-faced, looking as if he would burst.

'What kind of up-bringing are you giving this child that he displays such rudeness to his grandfather? Such cheek.'

Merv and I stared at each other aghast.

'But he's a little boy…' said Merv. 'He's excited…he doesn't mean anything.'

'You've brought him up to be deliberately cheeky to his grandfather!'

I stood in front of my father as he shouted, unconsciously forming a barrier between him and my two excited children whose faces were now dropping rapidly into fear.

He turned and left, shaking his fist. The children were crying. My family Chanukah party was ruined.

From then I deliberately began resisting the religious call to 'honour my father and my mother', reducing the telephone calls to my father to only a couple of times a year – usually running up to the Jewish New Year. Even then I had to pluck up the courage to call him. I knew he would be disagreeable at best. He never rang me. I would ring him and wish him the best for the following year and to be 'well over the fast', but I would always be greeted with, 'And to what do I owe the honour of this call?' or, worse, 'What do you want – you've hardly bothered the whole year, I could be dead by now!'

I would put down the receiver and sob.

Chapter 16

Mazaltov and Simentov

1984. A time of reconciliation and the year of Joe's *barmitzvah*. To a Jewish family this is a very special time. It marks a watershed in a young boy's life. At the age of thirteen he has to read and sing his *Maphtir* and *Haphtorah* – two large pieces of Hebrew script – in front of relations and friends and this act denotes his progress from childhood to manhood according to the Jewish religion; a daunting task for any child but particularly complicated for Joe, being dyslexic. Halfway through his year of study, we discovered that he was learning the wrong portion of the law and he had to start over again with only six months to go. As he relearned his new section, I listened to his singing and made lists.

I had decided to cater the function myself, hiring a marquee – a stressful undertaking but with no local kosher caterer it seemed the answer. Anyway, hadn't I catered everyone else's party? The plans grew with the numbers of guests. Forty people for an intimate Friday night, just close family and friends from away, which would be a traditional Friday supper – melon, home-made soup, roast chicken or fish with rice and vegetables and an apple pie, poached fruit, chocolate mousse, lemon tea and black coffee. The next day we planned to receive one hundred and fifty for lunch and two hundred for supper. One of the dietary strictures of the Jewish religion is that between setting a meat meal and a milk meal, it is necessary to change all the dishes including the cooking utensils, cutlery etc. As no normal household possesses this number of dishes, it is essential to hire new sets. So we hired new sets and paid a professional chef to present the food and oversee the specially hired staff on the day. Nothing was left to chance. I was determined that all 'my people' would enjoy a magical meal. First, assorted smoked fish with toast or homemade vegetable soup, then roast stuffed turkey breast and roast chicken, followed by a dessert where a martini glass was filled with rosé-wine-poached nectarines, layered with Advocaat, topped with an iced zabaglione, and decorated with home-made chocolate spirals. For the evening I cooked twenty salmons. I had ordered ten large but the wholesalers sent twenty small which increased the workload. They were laid out decorated with salads: potato salad, carrot orange and raisin salad, cucumber and dill salad, and a green salad. Then there was a buffet table of home-made desserts: apple pies and chocolate roulade and pavlovas filled with cream and fruit. I made all the bread to accompany the meal and with Merv's help decorated the top table and the buffet table with autumn fruits and flowers – pumpkins and squashes, and other magnificent harvest fruits: apples, pears, plums, and imported peaches and grapes. And of course there was a special birthday cake to make and decorate.

As I cooked, Joe sat in the kitchen and sang his portion of the law. I was proud. It was a difficult undertaking for him and he was determined to succeed. Then suddenly the months were gone – all the weeks of preparation finished. New clothes were purchased, the photographer engaged, and I made all the table decorations to match the lemon drapes of the marquee. We planned the table plan meticulously, placing my father far away from the various people he did not speak to, in the hope that he would be pleasant.

The morning of Joe's *barmitzvah* arrived, crisp and dry with the sound of a few November birds waking up a grey dawn. Just before we left for the synagogue, I checked that all was ready. The chef had arrived with his staff. The chilled food was waiting for assembly, the marquee looked wonderful and all the tables were perfect with their decorations. Nothing could go wrong.

As we left, I smelt toast, and assumed that the waitresses must be making themselves some breakfast. Little did I know that the heaters around the marquee, which had been lit early to ensure that the temporary room was warm, had set fire to the coconut matting flooring. Fortunately, it was discovered and dealt with before creating too much damage. Just a curious smell lingered over the day's proceedings, especially where the dark patches had stained the temporary carpet.

The ceremony was beautiful. My wonderful Aunty Essie had come from Israel specially for the event and sat next to me in the synagogue. We were surrounded by other members of our family and close friends. All the male members of our family were called up to say a blessing. My only regret was that my mother was not there to see her grandson on his big day. Joe was called up to read the law. Unusually tall for his age, and pale, he looked stiff and awkward in his new suit. I felt the tears prick and swallowed a large lump growing in my throat as he began to sing in a clear voice. I followed each word with him and, finally, he slumped back in the seat with an audible gasp of relief. The congregation laughed and shouted *Mazaltov* and I cried with delight and satisfaction at his success. Despite all his problems he had accomplished so much.

After the *Kiddush* in the synagogue – a celebratory small meal with a blessing over cholla-bread and wine, with cake and titbits – we walked back to the house confident that the difficult part of the day was behind us and that the rest could be devoted to celebration. Eventually all the guests were seated, and another member of the family said a blessing over the bread. Merv made a speech welcoming our friends and the finale of the meal would be the desserts and Joe's speech. This was his other major hurdle. When the time came he spoke, still in a child's voice, thanking parents and friends for coming and for their presents, telling jokes about his sister and finishing his performance by singing the whole of *G-d Save the Queen* in a Donald Duck voice, which had his audience crying with laughter. As he was in full flight, my father shouted to his wife to leave with him. Joe coped. He was used to his grandfather's tantrums. I laughed with embarrassment, but sobbed inwardly. My friends noticed and tried to console me. but the hurt would not disappear. My father had just demonstrated his lack of interest in my children in the most public way he could.

The rest of the day went perfectly. The food was enjoyed and the celebration ended with hugs and kisses. But an ache of acute sadness clung to me like a parasite, nurtured by my disillusionment. Finally and regretfully, I decided that a normal relationship with my father was impossible. That despite all my efforts to engage him and his new wife, he only wanted to damage my family's happiness.

So the cold war re-established itself, even stronger than before. I had always been the one who phoned. Now there was nothing. The children were used to scenes of tears after one of my father's visits, so they never asked me to invite him. They did not remember receiving gifts from him, or even a card on their birthday or *Chanukah*. Occasionally, after a row, he had stuffed a note into their hands but it was always given with bad grace. So there were no special memories linked with their important days.

Occasionally, in the synagogue or in the street, we would bump into each other, but now we were strangers. The relationship died like an un-watered plant.

People would come up to me in the street.

'Your father was rude to me!'

'Your father ignored me!'

'I'm so sorry, but I'm not my father,' I used to say. They seemed to think that in some way I was responsible for his rudeness.

My specially-loved uncle, my mother's brother, who had made a tortured way through concentration camps and emerged with a stronger faith, arrived from America with his daughter on a visit and we talked for hours about the situation. And about his sister.

'We could find Judith's book and get it published as a memorial to your mother,' he suggested in his glorious American drawl.

'That would be marvellous,' Merv and I agreed.

My uncle rang my father to ask if we could have the children's book.

'I sent it back to the illustrator. She's moved to Ireland or somewhere,' he said. 'And no, I haven't got her address.'

'Ask about the paintings…go on… ask about those.'

'The paintings…I burnt them…they are gone.'

So the years passed. Each time I saw my father he looked thinner and more drained. In one of our few meetings he told me that he was happy on his diet of oranges and meat and that he enjoyed looking slim. Now a qualified nutritionist, needing to make people well, I worried about the effect this faddy diet would have on his health. He still had not eliminated his cigarettes. I knew that this craziness would ultimately kill him. But he would never listen to me.

So it was no surprise when I heard that he had had a heart bypass. What was shocking to me was my stepmother's insistence that my father did not want to see me and that if I went to the hospital he would have me ejected. Hurt again, and trying to come to terms with this news, I waited to hear that he was improving and that maybe his brush with death would persuade him to reach out to a family that had always wanted him. But before we'd had a chance to come to terms with the first piece of news, we were called to the hospital with the report that he was dying. Apparently blood tests had revealed a particularly virulent form of leukaemia. We walked into the ward hearing only his choking for breath. He waved a claw fist at us and then shrank into his body shuddering and making growling animal sounds. This lasted for six hours until the doctor arrived and sedated him. He sank into a half sleep and, after a couple of hours, finally died. Yes, I did cry. I cried at the waste. At the whole damn situation. At the fact that I had never received an affectionate hug or a kiss from him or been told that I was loved, and that we had missed so much as a family. And that the children had never known the love of their grandparent.

As is the custom in the Jewish religion, the funeral was organised as quickly as possible. I realised I would have to go back into the house I hated and the prospect filled me with huge trepidation.

We arrived early. At my stepmother's request the hearse would leave from the house. I had made cake for after the service but was terrified to put it in the kitchen – to even go into the kitchen. But I forced myself. Within the familiarity of the room, nothing had changed; there was a coldness, but also a feeling of anticipation. Merv walked into the lounge and after speaking to my father's wife and checking whether she was alright, he shouted out in the middle of the open lounge: 'Look Geoff, I know that you do not want all these people here, most of all me. But If I don't lift all these Persian carpets off the polished floor, someone is going to have an accident.'

He rolled the carpets away as the people began to arrive.

My mother's best friend arrived and said, 'I never liked coming back here once your mother had died. It was as if she was still here but so unhappy…'

A few minutes later, someone called, 'The hearse is here.'

My stepmother and I walked slowly down the small winding path to the gate. As I walked, I was suddenly pushed forcibly out of the way. There was no one there. But as I reached the hearse I saw, out of the corner of my eye, something I can only describe as a piece of golden gauze that joined another and extended and moved up to the sky. It was quick but beautiful. I walked back to the house shaken and slowly moved from room to room. There was no coldness any more.

My mother's friend said, 'It's fine, isn't it? It's as if Judith has left now…she's happy at last. She's gone from this house.'

I walked into the kitchen. There was no coldness. Just a kitchen with the soft touches of my mother's hand, the design of the place exactly as it had been: the Italian plates, bought on a holiday years before, arranged on a shelf, a large gold and bronze vase I gave to them when I was a child, which had cost me months of saving.

My mother had left the house at last. I convinced myself that I had imagined the last few minutes and that I was just trying to console myself. But the image would not go. I telephoned the rabbi the next day and asked him to come round. He was with me at nine o'clock.

'What did I see? Please help me. I'm sure that in some way I saw my mother and my father departing.'

He was not surprised and told me that this was what Jews believed. That before the advent of electricity, it was usual to see ancestors standing behind and about a person in the synagogue. I have to live with what I saw and particularly with what I felt, and that was a strong push – though no one was there.

It is comforting to believe that we do meet our loved ones again.

Sadly my parents are buried in separate cemeteries.

I have very few of my parent's possessions. I had to ask my stepmother for my mother's candlesticks, to pass on to my daughter, and the *Kiddush becher* that I bought them to give to my son. I have my mother's art books, her cake tins. My stepmother has the rest.

231

But I have all the memories.

Chapter Seventeen

And Do I Wear My Mother's Shoes?

There are times when I worry my nails do not look perfect, that the dishes in the kitchen cupboards are not sitting like soldiers. That the very, very darkest reaches of the fridge have not seen a cloth and been washed out properly for a whole week or that I am just sitting, maybe with a magazine, and not doing anything valuable – wasting time. Then I wonder: am I turning into my mother? Our voices are the same, that funny kink in the front of our hair is the same. In photographs hers is always there despite the straighteners and the setting lotions. The same too are our hands, the long nail beds, the parts I like about myself that I watch in pleasant animation as they run over the keyboard of my PC, inherited by my daughter and now so evident in my little granddaughters, with their perfect and beautiful gesticulation.

Nature or nurture provided me with her passion for Edward Elgar, Tchaikovsky and Rachmaninoff – I added the Bruch, the Puccini and Verdi. She also instilled a love of books – heavy French Impressionist art books were venerated in the house. Again I added Pre-Raphaelite and a very non-Jewish passion for icons and Byzantine art.

But to what extent is my psychology and my physiology like my mother? Why is the discussion so relevant? Because the fear exists in me that eventually I may become her. I might inherit her love of the tapping-bones symphony and the smooth touch of paper skin over the concave hollows of an empty stomach.

Could I fall in love with the needle on the scales? No chance, you might think. With my experiences and with my past? And yet, sadly, after the birth of my second child, hating my plumpness, hating the residual stomach fold lying underneath the stretch of T-shirt, I became its slave. That is part of the reason for writing this book. To show how even when there are numerous warnings, even when there is an acute and painful personal awareness of the problem of anorexia, of the skeleton's rattle, and the scythe of the grim reaper harvesting another, it may still possess you.

You run up and down the stairs – ten before breakfast. Twenty sit-ups before lunch. Another ten stair runs before supper. The euphoria of beating the fat is good. The buzz of endorphins can carry your body and mind to another place. And that is how it deceives. The disease pretends to be your friend. Your salvation. It wears the mask of *good* and *healthy*. All the magazines and papers recite the same religious words. And when a few pounds drop and you slip, slip, into a smaller dress size, you feel so triumphant that it is automatic to think yes, yes, I can do this! Another dress size. Go lower, go lower. If you pause, the nagging beat of the sickness forces you to continue. You miss the helter-skelter slide down the scales to the next level. You need the gasp of admiration from your friends. It becomes tempting to go lower, lower. The scales become not a guide but a signal of your mood for the day. Weigh in the morning; down is a happy day, level will just be about alright, but if that needle shows a gain then it will be a bad day. At this stage you are in danger.

We were sitting on the deck of a rented house-boat on the Thames. A week's holiday, idyllic time spent together, and the end of another beautiful day. Our two children were finally sleeping in their bunks below deck. Boating is an up-close experience. Everything moves into a different focus so that the images of life are seen as if through a magnifying glass. A late dusk, us relaxing outside, watching the sun melt over the watery horizon. It was such a pleasure just sitting close-together. I'd dished out our suppers. We sat with a bowl each. His was home-cooked pasta covered with tomato sauce and topped with grated cheese: mine was boiled marrow with a tiny drop of the tomato sauce. I was happy that I was wearing a size ten pair of trousers from C&A. I was aware of the bones of my knees under the thinness of the fabric. It felt good.

'Is that all you're eating?' He said.

'I don't want any more. I'm full.'

'Impossible! You can't be full on that.'

The water lapped, rocking our bodies in a gentle motion and the sun sent layers of gilded light to change the river into rippled silk, patterned with black silhouetted ducks and swans. Like sequin glitter in the dusk.

The next day I was preparing breakfast. My heart seemed to be beating faster and I dropped a box of porridge on the carpet. The flakes scattered everywhere. Merv was watching my hands shaking and suddenly recognised my devils.

'Look at you!' he shouted. 'You're crazy, your hands are shaking so much. You're killing yourself. Love, if you don't stop, and stop right now, you are going to go the same way as your mother. Stop, please, or I'm going to lose you.'

I never realised. I had been changing into her likeness and yet I was outside of the picture. She was staring at me reflected in the water, happy. Sharing my pleasure at the spareness of flesh, calling me with dead fingers to join her. But he and the little ones were my reality, and Merv's anger a shaking, shocking alarm to return to the world of eating and pounds and tasting foods and to abandon the god of the needle. At the end of that week, leaving the boat to return home, I packed the toys, the left-over packets of food, clothes, and my skinny identity. All the way home in the car I tried to think how I would cope with the new me. I thought maybe he would have forgotten our conversation. But no. As soon as we arrived the weighing scales were put out with the dustbins for the next day, and retrieved by a delighted bin-man to pass on to his wife or some other disciple.

Merv saved my life on that sweet rocking boat.

Postscript

Remembrance

Writing this book has caused me huge anxiety. It is almost as if my mother has sat next to me watching and listening to my words, sometimes arguing with them or trying to hide them out of respect for my father and to save the feelings of others. I feel her body close to mine – a tissue thin spectre, containing an immense spirit. My reality is the past, she has never left me, and sometimes when I hear a piece of music, or particularly on the Passover when we as a family argue over the proper format of the *Seder* and which *matzo* to eat with lettuce or *harozeth*, I hear her beautiful voice singing, as if she is with me. I have agonised for hours over whether I should continue writing. I am exposing the very essence of someone precious to me. But each time I stop I feel I have to continue. There are millions of people in the world – young carers, older women with dysfunctional eating problems, and their carers, who need a voice, and if this book helps them to be heard then my mother's death has not entirely been the futile desecration that it was at the time. On holiday this year, after a painful illness, I felt I experienced a crisis. That she was angry with me. I talked with Merv for hours over one café Americano after another, in a quiet Italian garden, in the middle of *Ferragosto* when all around me were partying. Ultimately, I felt as if I was given permission to talk. That I have been given the chance to speak in her absence and for her. To shout in her place about the small cruelties that she experienced every day – the intolerances, the swift looks, the hidden laughter covered by mocking hands – and to restore the respect due to her that had somehow evaporated. She was a very talented and beautiful lady.

So now, all these years later, have I buried the guilt with those poor tired bones? Why should it have taken me sixteen years to look at a headstone engraved with my mother's name? And why write this book now?

Firstly, the sheer bloody waste of a wonderful woman whose presence haunts me every day. So much so that when I see an old photograph, unless it is from the very early years, I cry. It still hurts as if it was yesterday. I am a grandmother and I would like to show my beautiful granddaughters pictures of their late great-grandmother but I am afraid that they may have nightmares if they look at her face. So instead of proudly showing my family in sweet old albums, the photos are stashed away at the back of the drawer. The legend and the roots are damaged.

I still acknowledge the guilt and absorb it as mine. I enclose it as a child in school curves elbows around a secret painting or writing. Logically I know I cannot be blamed for the tragedy. As a child I tried so desperately to prevent it, offering my own body to some god of deals – the one that says, 'If you do this?' I promised always to say the prayers, attend synagogue, never travel on the Sabbath, learn by rote the formulae of a religion, perform all the rites, and in some way expect us to be saved. But of course I could not maintain that daily level of commitment.

All of this writing is coloured with a prayer to refrain from self abuse, which we do continuously: 'I'm so fat, look at my thighs! I'm a bloody pig with food. I hate myself in a bathing costume!' Women constantly criticise themselves. The child listens to the one who is supposed to know – her mother – and learns the habit by example. The small child sits in her ballet school and examines the breadth of her childish legs, she sits in the back of the car on the way home from school with a pretend phone in her hand and listens to her mother making calls –

'What are you going to wear? Oh you're so lucky, you're so thin. You can wear anything. I'll have to wear black. It hides my bulges – masks the belly – covers my bum.'

Thinness remains the god of glamour, the god of control, popularity and success. Thinness trips along on her finest stilettos with her bone hips exposed though layers of fabric, waving her stick arms and calling like the Pied Piper for new children to follow. Sadly they do. But this is a false god. This is a god that draws to the grave. Thinness laughs as her new charges refuse their food, spit out, vomit in secret and spin in front of mirrors to look at backs where a bony spine chatters, still exclaiming that they are so fat.

All my life I have been caught in a sticky web of confusion, the cruelties, the losses, and the pains of that life, the ghastly consequences of an ugly disease that, make no mistake, I have inherited. Oh yes, I have thrown away the weighing scales and abandoned tape measures. I no longer feel annihilated if my jeans are tight, but still steady my resolve to restore the shape. I worry about my children and my grandchildren's inheritance. I overreact, fearful a childish belly may be mistaken for weight gain. Anxious in case they absorb commenting words, words that pronounce judgement. Because they may then look at their bodies and learn dissatisfaction and discover the hideous routes of change.

What is positive, however, is that at last, after trying to cope for over half a century, I have at last arrived at a place of understanding from where I can at least face the pain – confront the monster in its cave and begin to fight. And I hope that through my grief and my progression to this place of knowledge, I can help others who are still suffering. Maybe by seeing these tragic photographs and hearing the truths, they will be frightened into realising that this sickness

is real. It will kill slowly and painfully, and it distorts the
feelings and personalities of the loved and loving.

Judith & Geoff in happier days

Red Stilettos
By Ruth Joseph

A sensational collection of quality short stories.

*"An astonishingly honest, real and utterly moving collection
of short stories that haunt you long after reading."*
Western Mail

*"Crisply written portrayals of human encounters with the
occasional Jewish flavour..."* **The Jewish Chronicle**

*"Sensitively-written, Ruth Joseph touches on some serious
contemporary issues in her delightful short stories. An
emerging talent worth watching."*
Carole Matthews, International Bestselling Novelist

*"Strong, passionate writing. This is a new, rich, exciting
talent."* **Catherine Merriman, Novelist**

ISBN 0954489977   RRP £7.99

The Boy I Love
By Marion Husband

"Compelling & sensual. Well written..."
PENNY SUMMER

"A vivid and accomplished debut; Marion Husband explores the morality of wartime Britain with intelligent and compassionate insight."
DEBBIE TAYLOR, EDITOR, MSLEXIA

The story is set in the aftermath of World War One. Paul Harris, still frail after shellshock, returns to his father's home and to the arms of his secret lover, Adam. He discovers that Margot, the fiancée of his dead brother, is pregnant and marries her through a sense of loyalty. Through Adam he finds work as a schoolteacher, while setting up a home with Margot he continues to see Adam.

Pat Morgan, who was a sergeant in Paul's platoon, runs a butcher's shop in town and cares for his twin brother Mick, who lost both legs in the war. Pat yearns for the closeness he experienced with Paul in the trenches.

Set in a time when homosexuality was 'the love that dare not speak its name' the story develops against the background of the strict moral code of the period. Paul has to decide where his loyalty and his heart lies as all the characters search hungrily for the love and security denied them during the war.

ISBN 1905170009   RRP £6.99

Paper Moon
By Marion Husband

The sequel to *The Boy I Love*

"This is an extraordinary novel. Beautifully controlled pacy prose carefully orchestrates the relationships of many well drawn characters and elegantly captures the atmosphere of England in 1946...This novel is perfect."
Margaret Wilkinson

Paul's son Bobby escapes Thorp to become a Spitfire pilot during World War Two. When his plane is shot down he learns to come to terms with the terrible burns he suffers even as his past returns to haunt him.

Paper Moon is a passionate love story set in 1946 that explores how the sins of the fathers can have far-reaching effects on their sons.

ISBN 1905170149   RRP £6.99
AVAILABLE APRIL 2006

Raffy's Shapes
By Tamar Hodes

Bizarrely beautiful, pure escapism. It's simply wonderful.

Raphaella Turner is a best-selling painter who lives beside a lake. Inside her cottage, everything is white. When she is not creating her huge, brightly coloured abstract paintings, she swims in the lake and changes shape. Sometimes she is a bird or sometimes a fish. Unknown to Raphaella, her real mother, Martha, lives on the other side of the lake with her husband Richard and four sons. Martha also changes shape as did her mother Helga, escaping from a difficult life in Nazi Germany as a Jew, and an unhappy marriage.

The title *Raffy's Shapes* refers to Raphaella's collection of shapes in jars, her paintings, her shape-changing, and the two sand-world's she creates, one to live in and one to draw away the unwelcome attention of the people who want to understand and cash in on her genius. The novel explores, among others themes such as deceit and truth, the complex nature of creativity and the desire to make shapes.

ISBN 1905170173   RRP £6.99
AVAILABLE JULY 2006